Emotional Power

How to Understand and Use Your Emotions to Propel Yourself to a Better Life

Dr. Karen R. Perkins

Published by HeartWork Publishing, LLC
7777 N Wickham Rd, # 12-247
Melbourne, FL 32940
www.MotivationalPress.com
www.HeartWorkPublishing.com

Manufactured in the United States of America.

ISBN: 978-1-62865-235-2

Dedication

To my sister, Heather, for inspiring me to stay tuned in to my emotions.

To my phenomenal husband, Darwin, for encouraging me on a daily basis, being my co-conspirator, and the main editor of the content of this work.

Contents

Acknowledgements

M Y LIFE IS TRULY BLESSED AND I AM ETERNALLY GRATEFUL TO BE surrounded by great friends and family.

To my children: You inspire me daily. Your talents, your strengths, your kindness and love for others are traits you should always be proud of! Thanks for believing in your crazy and sometimes unconventional mother! Your faith in me encourages me to continue to strive to improve.

To my son, Spenser: A special thanks goes to you for the endless hours at the drafting board, creating, modifying, and perfecting the artwork and designs for so many of my projects.

To my sister, Julie, and my two closest friends, Janice and Karen: Thank you for being my biggest cheerleaders! I know no matter what the day holds, no matter the time or distance, I can count on you for love, support and praise! Your belief in me is touching and appreciated.

To all my friends: This book is filled with examples and life stories that would not have been possible to recount without the open and wonderful friendships that allowed you to share so much. Thank you for your friendship and allowing me to share these stories.

To my friend and publishing genius Ronda Taylor, and my clean up editor, Karen Sebastian: Thank you for your guidance and patience. It is always comforting to know that you will be there all the way from the big decisions to the minute details while making sure things are gramatically correct. Karen, thank you for the extra hours helping me clarify my thoughts, fixing grammar, and helping the words flow smoothly.

To Dr. Tony Alessandra: Your expertise and collective works inspired my passion for this subject. I have been a student of yours throughout my adult life. It is a great honor to me that you are willing to take your time to share your thoughts regarding this work.

To Darwin, the love of my life: Foremost, I must acknowledge your dedication, love, and support that you give so freely. Love, the day we met was a turning point for eternal bliss and happiness in my life. With you, I have experienced more love and joy than I ever imagined possible. Each day brings a deeper sense of passion and tenderness. I want to thank you for the countless hours and immense efforts spent brainstorming, reading, editing, and polishing this book. All I am today and all I'll be tomorrow, is because of your devotion. I adore you MOTL.

Foreword

"I don't want to be at the mercy of my emotions. I want to use them, to enjoy them, and to dominate them."

—Oscar Wilde, *The Picture of Dorian Gray*

IN THE CLASSIC NOVEL, THE PICTURE OF DORIAN GRAY, THE ETERnally young Dorian Gray declares complete dominance over his emotions. To take Gray's words at face value, one should not be at the mercy of one's emotions, only dominate them. As Mr. Gray finds out too late, peace in life comes from balance.

Dr. Karen Perkins' *Emotional Power* teaches that emotions let us know if we are comfortable with a situation, or if we are not. Emotions are our guides, our warning signals, and our rewards. Emotions are to be proudly used as the tools they are; not to be feared, shunned, or ignored. Emotions are to be used.

I was delighted to read this new volume from Dr. Perkins on this subject. Her use of personal stories and anecdotes brings a normally overwhelming topic to life. From the first uplifting story about Pearl, to the final gripping story about Heather, every chapter entertains, builds, and teaches the step-by-step approach you will use to assess, address, and enhance your interactions with others (and yourself).

Karen takes us through the steps to identify our emotions, embrace them, enjoy them, feel them, understand them, and then to use them as a powerful tool towards personal strength. Unlike Dorian Gray, whose goal is the domination of his emotions meant to only experience pleasure, Karen teaches us how to find true power, comfort, peace and pleasure in most areas of our lives through understanding ourselves.

As Socrates philosophy states, "Know Thyself." The key to success is embedded in an understanding of self and in providing the positive service to others that only someone like you can. Karen shows the path to unleash the power behind each emotion, embrace, harness, and utilize that same power for our own benefit and for the benefit of others.

While we all use and deal with emotions, not all of us have developed our natural skillsets to positively control the responses we have to events in our lives. Karen walks us through both the science and the logic behind emotions, and then provides examples, tools, and opportunities to enhance these natural skillsets by recognizing and acting positively when events in our life trigger emotional responses.

Emotional Power is a pivotal step in understanding, embracing, and excelling at being the most powerful person you can be. I knew as soon as I read Pearl's story that I had to read more. Pearl, a spunky character who arrives in the first few pages of this inspiring book, introduces the power of one's emotions in a manner that intrigued me. Pearl's story illustrates what it's like to stand tall where others may have crumbled, and to stand tall when we're expected by others and even ourselves to crumble. By standing tall as she did, Pearl demonstrated emotional victory both personally and professionally.

Karen leads you through the process of learning about the role emotions play in your life. From linking scientific research on emotions to personal self-discovery of those emotions in yourself, she identifies the steps to follow and pitfalls to avoid in coming to grips with the way you personally deal with events in your life. She points out that most of our emotional responses are ones that we have learned over time and they are ingrained in ourselves until we believe they are the only natural response. She shows that all of our responses can, with a little effort, be rethought, relearned, and then effectively channeled to provide more positive outcomes.

As Founder and CEO of Assessments24x7.com—a company that offers online 360° assessments—I am credited as being a leading expert on behavioral profiling. I love Karen's unique approach in describing the various personalities and how they are perceived from the other personality viewpoints. Her way of conveying the information for each personality style is intriguing and educational.

Emotional Power will help you discover simple, yet effective, tools and tactics to master each of the five components of emotional power: Awareness, Attitude, Empathy, Social Skills, and Emotional Management. It is both a primer and an advanced guide to understanding the role of emotions in your life and to dealing with the four major behavioral styles.

—Dr. Tony Alessandra,
Author of *The Platinum Rule* and *Charisma*

Introduction

E VER SINCE WE WERE YOUNG CHILDREN, MOST OF US FELT THE IN-
tense power of emotion. Do you remember being a child and feeling
so overwhelmed by your feelings that you had a meltdown, started crying, or threw something? Most of us can remember instances like that.
And, most of us can remember getting in trouble for it at least once or
twice! Some of us still do!

Today, we live in a culture that tends to think of emotions—
particularly negative emotions—as something bad; something that
indicates inherent flaws in one's strength or one's character. Simply put,
it's not acceptable to be too emotional. This is especially true in the
workplace!

The Purpose of Emotions

Have you ever stopped to think about the REAL purpose of emotions? In my years as a consultant, I have come to realize that emotions
hold tremendous power and energy. Some of the greatest changes in
our world come from the power of emotions such as:

- The passion to right a wrong
- Anger to fight an injustice
- The joy of success.

These are all intense emotions that are used for good. They propel a
successful person or society forward.

An Emotion is Energy in Motion

Sadly, though, many of us don't know how to actually *use* our emotions. We're uneducated on our own emotional powers, their purpose

and their value. Some of us are hijacked by intense feelings and then stuck with all these strong emotions with no idea how to channel them into something constructive. So often we have no idea how to use the Energy in Motion; we fail to see that our Emotions can be a positive energy.

That's why I wrote this book. Everyone who has feelings —and that is pretty much everyone—can learn to harness the power of their emotions. It's through harnessing this power that we can propel ourselves to a state of mind that leads to our greatest successes.

Wait! That Was My Idea!

Here's a simple example of harnessing your emotional power: Let's say that you attend a team meeting. You've already had a couple of rough days and you're not in a very good mood when you get to this meeting. You diligently try to put your negative feelings aside as you share your ideas with the team.

One of the team members says, "That will never work. The client won't go for it." You become irritated but don't say anything. Ten minutes later Ted, a coworker that you don't particularly care for, offers an idea that is identical to one you gave last week. Last week that same idea was shot down in a fairly convincing fashion. However, when Ted, your annoying colleague, suggested it this week, the team loved the idea. Now your anger is starting to rise and your temper is about to boil over. What do you do?

I once saw someone in a meeting stand up, throw his notebook across the table, and stomp out of the room slamming the door behind him. Clearly, that's not an effective way to harness your emotional power. In a situation like this, do you think there may be something you can do to maintain your temper and actually TRANSFORM the power of that emotion into something good? Yes there is. It is possible (and desirable) to manage your emotions—good and bad—and use them to give you creative energy, solve problems and create lasting relationships.

While we'll get into specific techniques for managing emotions later on, to maintain control and move forward productively in this particular meeting, you might say, "Ted, I'm so glad you agree with what I proposed last week. Perhaps we could work together to strengthen this idea further."

This is much better! This simple statement allows you to take credit for your idea, while allowing the other person to retain their dignity. This enhances the chances of that person, as well as the other people in the group, working with you in a more positive manner in the future.

The Pearl of Wisdom

Many years ago, when I was still relatively new to management, I worked with a phenomenal woman named Pearl. Pearl gave me one of the greatest gifts I've ever received. I now identify this as one of the turning points in my life. You see, Pearl was a woman of great emotional power and strength. When you looked at this wonderful little old lady you probably would not consider her very powerful. But she was. This is the lesson I learned.

Pearl and I were put together on a team with several strong team-mates, which in this case, happened to all be men. This was an organization that had very few women in leadership and the few they had either were deemed "aggressive," or were dismissed altogether. Pearl didn't fit into the first category and worked persistently to keep from being trampled in the second one. The company was struggling and teams were given the challenge of finding a way to survive and thrive. We worked diligently on creating an option that would best meet the needs of the organization. We tossed around possibilities for a few days then Pearl came up with a fabulous idea. Details were gathered and the outline molded. All of us felt good about the direction it would take us as a team and as an organization. The original idea, however, was Pearl's brainchild. She asked to lead the presentation to the board.

The day of the presentation arrived. Several other teams gave their presentations and did a good job. We were all a little anxious. Future careers and decisions depended upon the presentations. When our turn arrived, Pearl stood and began to outline our team's information. She uttered a few sentences and then she began to cry. The tears rolled down her cheeks and her voice quivered and cracked. We thought it was over. The men on the team looked at me with an accusatory look as if to say, "We knew you women couldn't handle this." As I looked at Pearl, my mind was screaming, "What are you doing? You are killing us!" Pearl, that wonderful little old lady, knew the power behind her conviction and, instead of crumbling on the spot, relied on the power of her emotions.

No, she didn't let our expressions of horror set her back. Instead, she harnessed the emotions she was experiencing and demonstrated what True Emotional Power looks like. See, she didn't cry that day to be powerless or manipulative. She did, however, use the unexpected tears to her benefit. She used them as a launching point for the importance of what she was saying. So instead of trying to hide her tears or apologize for them, she simply acknowledged them.

She gracefully stopped speaking when her voice was cracking and looked at the rest of us and simply stated, "Ladies, Gentleman, you can see that I feel strongly about this proposal, please ignore my tears and let's focus on the facts." Then she continued to speak. Soon after, the tears started to dry up and her voice stopped quivering. She showed tremendous power and strength and was honest with herself and others about her emotions.

Communication Is the Key

How many times have we been told that showing emotions is showing weakness? It's a common belief that if we get emotional, we've lost control. This is simply not true! Our emotions EXIST to propel us forward—to take us to the next level in life. Emotions are the POWER that drives growth. And that's what this program is about.

In life, there are two types of communication: Internal and External. Internal Communication is called Programming —1500 words per minute, and hundreds of pictures, whizzing through your brain telling you who you are, who you aren't, what you can be, what you can do, what you can have. You determine your own internal communication by reprogramming what you allow yourself to believe and think. You must begin supplementing them with positive influences and positive thoughts, eliminating the negative self-talk before it takes root. Positive thoughts will change your programming. Positive programming leads to emotional strength.

External Communication is called Influence—it is the ability to communicate with other people in such a way they want to give you what you want. You develop positive external communication by developing your own personal social skills. Later in the program you will learn appropriate ways to develop social skills that will benefit you as well as others.

Everyone, including you, has been taught since youth what someone deemed as socially acceptable behavior towards others. This comes at the expense of our own positive programming. Negative programming has become a common societal practice. We are constantly bombarded with politically correct phrases like the following:

- Be humble.
- They think they are so great (said in an accusatory way).
- Who do they think they are?
- Don't be so competitive.
- You are no better than the next guy.
- You need to lose weight, be more attractive, sacrifice your time, and money, etc.

Any one of these comments can be valid at any given time. But when they are used as a general catch phrase, they become a sticky substance that will glue us to negative programming.

Shift Your Perceptions. Shift Your Thoughts.

Your programming, both positive and negative, directly affects your thought process. Your thought process is what determines your emotional state and your emotional behavior.

In the next chapters, we will cover:

- **Origin of Emotions:** How the science of emotion can help you to harness and utilize your emotions for great strength and motivation, both for yourself and for others.
- **Core Emotions as well as Primary and Secondary Emotions:** Learn about the Core Emotions as well as additional emotions most often felt, including Joy, Enthusiasm, and Fear.
- **Components of Emotional Power:** The concept of awareness and the key to understanding yourself and others.
- **Emotional Space:** What it is and the five steps to using emotional space effectively.
- **How Your Attitude Affects You:** The power of your attitude and how a positive attitude can lead to success and greater self-esteem.

- **The Power of Empathy:** We will define Empathy and discuss how it affects those around you.
- **Building Successful Social Skills:** Learn a simple model to help you understand the different kinds of people and how you can interact with each of them. We'll talk about Peacocks, Owls, Lambs, and Lions.
- **Different Communication Styles:** Learn what to say to inspire action and understanding in each style discussed.
- **Managing Your Emotions:** Discover five steps—including how to manage your physical reactions.
- **Identifying How You Experience Emotions:** Identify how YOU personally experience emotions. Do you cry? Does your voice change? Do you blush, laugh, shrug?
- **Identifying Your Core Values:** Identify your core values. Being true to your personal core values is the best way to manage stress
- **Instant Calming Sequences (ICS's):** Learn easy ways to modify your reaction to short-term stress along with long-term fixes.
- **The Five Fundamentals of Laughter:** Learn what they are. Learn the value of having a life plan.

By the end of this book, you'll have been introduced to all the tools you need to harness your emotional power and you'll be ready to use them to shape your life into what you really want it to be.

Are you ready to get started?

Let's go!

CHAPTER 1

The Origin of Emotions

HAVE YOU EVER WONDERED ABOUT THE SCIENCE BEHIND EMO-tions or where your emotions actually come from?

The Amygdala

There is a small almond shaped section called the amygdala in your brain. The amygdala is the brain's specialist on emotional matters. As you think, listen, or talk, your thoughts flow through this part of the brain. The amygdala links thoughts to emotions and then assigns a physical reaction to each emotion.

So, for example, if you start thinking about a cute baby, the amygdala assigns an emotion to that thought. This thought may be happiness or the joy of wonder. A physical action, such as smiling, occurs once that thought is paired up with an emotion.

Many people tell me, "Karen, I can't control my emotions. They just well up in me and I can't control them!" While you may not be able to control the end result, you can control the thoughts that started you on that path.

If you think, for example, about how your boss is a jerk and is always blaming you for things that go wrong, your emotions will be negative. You can change your thoughts if you don't want those negative emotions.

Reframe

Replace negative with positive. Start thinking about how lucky you are to have a job in the first place, or remind yourself how happy you are that you don't have to be like your boss (or live with him). Then, your amygdala can attach feelings of gratitude to these thoughts instead of the negativity that would surely follow "the boss is a jerk" thought.

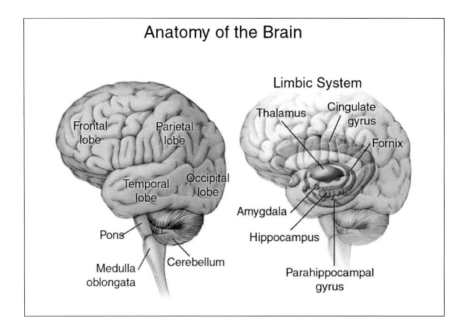

In order to do this, you must create a mental shift. This is when you allow yourself to frame your thoughts differently. As an example, how about a shift from a belief that something has happened on purpose, to the possibility that it may have been an accident.

Here's another example. The other day I was driving down the freeway and I needed to change lanes. Being the responsible driver that I am, I looked over both shoulders, in the mirrors, and performed all the safety measures that we are taught exemplify a good driver. As I looked, no one was there, so I changed lanes. Sure enough, there was someone in my blind spot and now they were honking angrily and giving me that one-finger wave that indicates that they are unhappy with what I just did. I was waving apologetically, with all four fingers and my thumb, to let him know that I was sorry and that it honestly was not intentional. From the honking and dirty looks, I'm sure my wave of apology didn't help the other driver feel any better about what had just happened.

Something happened about 30 seconds later once I was safely back in my own lane. Someone cut ME off and my immediate emotion was anger! I'm thinking, "Idiot! Moron! Who taught you how to drive?" Suddenly, I realized what I was doing. I was acting like that driver who had gone out of their way to make my day miserable. I assumed and behaved as if this driver did it on purpose!

Instantly, I realized I was thinking—and was tempted to act—like the person I had cut off 30 seconds earlier. If I had cut them off accidentally, the chances were really good that this driver had done it accidentally as well. I stopped being angry once I reframed this event as an accident, instead of bad driving. Instead, I started to see how they might be as embarrassed as I was.

Practice Makes Permanent

It's important to note that my first reaction, truly, was anger. I didn't control that emotion, but I changed it by purposely creating a mental shift. Many of my thought processes have changed on a permanent basis by consciously practicing and using mental shifts. I still can experience an unfortunate chain of events when driving. My first thought now is, "That's embarrassing." I no longer take it personally or believe the other person is a jerk or an idiot. If it appears shortly thereafter that it was intentional, I then think, "How embarrassing to be them."

Nothing is Imaginary

Here's another example of how powerful the amygdala can be. Jan, a good friend of mine, is a specialist in stress management and gives talks across North America on this topic. Jan likes to have her audience imagine a roller coaster ride. Typically, there will be a couple of people in the audience who are terrified of roller coasters. You can tell almost immediately, who they are. Jan will say, "Hear the clink, clink, clink as the coaster's car goes higher and higher. Clink, clink, you are 50 feet. Clink, clink, 75 feet. Clink, clink, you are now a 100 feet in the air. The coaster comes to a complete standstill, and then, swish. You're plunging down. It speeds up. It jolts back and forth, as you quickly descend. It whips around a corner and pivots up on its side and spins and...."

You can see some people go pale. They will start to rock in their chairs. Their hands get sweaty and their heart palpitates. People will get nervous, yet, they are clearly in a seminar room where they are completely safe from the imaginary roller coaster. By imagining that roller coaster ride, they literally experience the same emotions, and sometimes physical reactions, they would have had if they were actually on the ride itself.

So, your thoughts have a great amount of power. The truth is, your amygdala simply does not know the difference between reality and make-believe. To the amygdala, everything you think is a reality.

The Neo-cortex

Another part of the brain that acts upon our emotions is the neo-cortex. The neo-cortex is the analytical part of the brain. It is commonly hypothesized that the neo-cortex does its work before the amygdala. That is, it presents the logical reasoning to the emotional driver, which then assigns an emotion to the event or thought.

You have a thought or were presented with an event. Your first reaction is just that—a reaction. You have no time to think it over or to justify your actions. An emotion is assigned. Then you get a chance to think about it.

I definitely disagree with that theory.

I'm going to suggest that to get the maximum benefit of your emotional brainpower, you really must put the neo-cortex and the amygdala together. Work them as one, in unison, rather than placing one before the other. If you place one before the other, you are putting yourself at risk for indecision, paralysis, false conclusions, and, perhaps quick, inappropriate reactions.

For instance, let's say you do put the neo-cortex first. You happen to be in the woods. You come across a big bear. The neo-cortex says, "Hmmm, that is a bear. Is it a brown bear, a black bear or a grizzly bear? Once I was told that a black bear and a brown bear actually are the same kind of bear. Let's see, with some bears, you are supposed to look big and others you look like a rock…" Okay, by now you have been eaten!!

On the other hand, if you put the amygdala first, the amygdala says RUN FROM THE BEAR! The instant, knee-jerk reaction typically doesn't tell you which way to run. Just RUN! Unfortunately, without a predetermined direction, you might run right into the bear itself, or worse yet, the bear's cubs! Neither of these would have good results.

Thinking without feeling isn't wise, but neither is feeling without thinking. If you can learn to work the two together the amygdala will say, "Run!" and the neo-cortex will say, "Run to your car and close the door!"

That example shows a BIG risk–a Bear–something that is life-threatening. We rarely know in advance that we are going to face a life-threatening event before the event begins. It's not wise to wait for these big events or BEARS as I sometimes refer to them, before learning to work the analytical and the emotional process simultaneously.

In the rest of this book, I will refer to major challenges as BEARS. So when you see the word BEAR, or you see things as major challenges, ask yourself, "Would I stand firm, would I run, or would I use a combination of the two for best results"?

Practice Partnership

Practice on the simple events and the little things as they happen. Plan to work the amygdala and neo-cortex together, on the common situations you face regularly or know will happen. By starting small and setting the habit or pattern of working them together, you will then start to forge a bond that allows the two to interact naturally, regardless of the situation.

Practice using your emotions and your analytical thoughts together to motivate yourself to move forward. Then when those big things or BEARS happen, your brain will open up to many more possibilities. Our brain has tremendously powerful abilities that are just waiting to be tapped. Tap into these abilities, even if only a little, and use them for your benefit.

Your Truth, Your Life

I'd like to tell you a true story about a young man named Nick Sitzman. Nick was a strong, young bull of a man who worked on a train crew. It seemed Nick had everything: a healthy body, tons of ambition, a wife, two children and many friends.

However, Nick had one major fault; he was a notorious worrier. He worried about everything and usually feared the worst.

One mid-summer day, the train crew was informed they could quit an hour early in honor of the foreman's birthday. Nick was accidentally locked in a refrigerator boxcar as the rest of the workmen left the site.

Poor Nick panicked. He banged and shouted until his fists were bloody and his voice was hoarse, but no one heard him. "If I can't get out of here, I will freeze to death," Nick thought.

Wanting to let his wife and family know exactly what had happened to him, Nick found a knife and began to etch words on the wooden floor. He wrote, "It's so cold that my body is getting numb. I'm going to sleep. These may be my last words."

The next morning a crew member slid open the heavy doors of the boxcar and found Nick dead. An autopsy revealed that every physical sign of his body indicated that he had frozen to death. Yet, the refrigeration unit of the boxcar was inoperative and the temperature inside indicated 55 degrees. That's cold, but not freezing. Had Nick killed himself simply by the power of worry?

Ask yourself the following question: what have I worried about unnecessarily? And, what kind of damage did I cause myself, or maybe even others, from the needless effects of my worrying?

As I said earlier, our thoughts go through the amygdala; the amygdala assigns both an emotion and a physical reaction. Our thoughts are a reality to the amygdala. It has been proven scientifically that our thoughts produce energy waves, and these energy waves attract like energy waves. If you have positive thoughts, you attract positive events and people. If you have negative thoughts, you repel positive events and positive people, and you attract negative ones.

Attraction: The Real Cause and Effect

Think about it, when you are in a good mood, a truly good mood, and somebody is negative, grumpy, and ornery, don't you want to avoid him or her like the plague? On the other side of that coin, if you are grumpy and ornery, and just not in a good mood yourself, don't you find yourself avoiding the positive people because you find their cheeriness downright annoying? On the other hand, maybe you avoid them because they are not allowing you to have your grumpy moment. This is known as the law of attraction. The law of attraction states that your thoughts will attract the things that you truly believe; the very things you think about.

Deborah, another friend of mine, always seemed to get a parking space right up front, wherever she went. It happened so often that people began to borrow her car just so they could park up front at the mall, grocery store, or wherever they needed to be.

I had the opportunity to travel with her on occasion. I noticed that when she pulled into any parking lot, she would say, "I've got a parking space right up front." And oddly enough, she always did. I, of course, am the person who always ended up parking in the back North 40 because there was never a parking space close when I pull into the lot.

After questioning her on how she got these spots over and over again, she declared it was all in the way we think. To illustrate her explanation, she gave me a challenge to change my own belief system. Deborah challenged me to change what I thought whenever I pulled into a parking lot. For the next 90 days, I was to say, "I have a parking space right up front."

I will be honest with you that when I first started doing this, I got a little sarcastic. "I've got a parking space right up front!" Okay, I got a lot sarcastic! Do you know what happened? I still parked in the North 40. I did not get a parking space right up front.

Belief vs. Wish

Deborah then said, "Karen, your sarcasm is declaring you don't believe you'll get a space. And because you are declaring disbelief, it is not going to happen. You are going to continue to park in the back until you get over that."

I mustered up all the energy I could. I started with a hesitant hope at first, and then later an avid belief and said, "I've got a parking space right up front." At first, in the back of my mind I still had that fear that I was lying to myself. But the front of my mind said, "Okay, I believe it. I believe it. I believe it."

An amazing thing started to happen. I began to park closer and closer and closer to the front. Eventually, I honestly began to believe it actually was true. I started to say with conviction, "I've got a parking space right up front!" And you know, before the 90 days were up, I got a parking space right up front, within the first three stalls, 95 to 98 percent of the time.

Do I believe the people who had been in those spaces, felt the positive energy coming from my thoughts, and felt an overwhelming need to run for their car and leave just so I could have a parking space?

No, I do not. What I believe is my mind opened up to the possibility that there might be something better than what I had, or even something different from where I was.

Belief Increases Probability

See, before my 90-day trial I believed there would never be anything close, so I gave up. I never looked and took the first space I saw. Now, I have come to realize that the people up front leave as often as the people in the back. Because I understand that truth, I drive around the parking lot one time, and one time only. And honestly, I do get a parking space right up front 95% to 98% of the time. My new belief allows me to take time to actually look for it. I find a better spot simply because I believe there will be a space, and I don't give up prematurely.

Your thoughts and beliefs actually do affect the facts and your outcomes. They sometimes drive the facts or, put another way, create possibilities, probabilities, or even impossibilities for you. Your facts affect your drive, which then affects your behavior. Your behavior will affect others' thoughts and the way people behave towards you.

This is where mental shifts, as we discussed earlier, are so critically important.

What is the key to creating that mental shift?

Awareness

Awareness is vital. You also need to learn to create the mental shift that opens your mind to other ways of seeing things. As you look for other possibilities, you begin to search for additional truth.

CHAPTER 2

The Core Levels of Emotions

BASICALLY, THERE ARE THREE LEVELS OF EMOTIONS. THERE ARE core emotions, then our primary emotions, and finally our secondary emotions.

Core Emotions

There are two core emotions that everyone shares: love and fear. At first thought, many believe it is love and hate, or love and anger. In truth, love's opponent is fear. Our positive emotions will typically stem from love while our negative emotions typically stem from unhealthy fear.

According to the Oxford Dictionary, love is an emotion of strong affection and personal attachment. Love is also said to be a virtue representing all human kindness, compassion and affection.

In English, love refers to a variety of different feelings and attitudes, ranging from pleasure ("I loved that meal") to interpersonal attraction ("I love my partner"). Love may also refer specifically to the passionate desire or a romantic love, to the emotional closeness of familial love, to the platonic love that defines friendship, to the profound oneness or devotion of religious love, or to a concept of love, that encompasses all of these feelings.

This diversity of uses and meanings, combined with the complexity of the feelings involved, makes love unusually difficult to define consistently. You can, however, trace almost all of your positive emotions and reactions back to the basics of love. In short, love is what makes you feel good inside.

Fear, on the other hand, is the opposing core emotion. Let's evaluate it. Fear is described as an emotion induced by a perceived threat that causes one to move quickly away from that perceived threat, and to sometimes hide from such threats. It is a basic survival mechanism occurring in response to a specific stimulus, such as pain or the threat of danger. In short, fear is the ability to recognize danger leading to an urge to confront it, or to flee from it. This is known as the fight-or-flight response. In extreme cases of fear, the freeze or paralysis response is typical. Fear can also lead to anxiety.

Frequently, fear results from specific behaviors of escape and avoidance. Anxiety is then a result of threats that are perceived to be uncontrollable or unavoidable. It is worth noting that fear usually relates to future events, such as worsening of a situation, or continuation of a situation that is unacceptable.

Fear can also be an instant reaction to something presently happening. All people have an instinctual response to potential danger, which is, in fact, important to the survival of all species.

Let's be clear on the strength of fear. You can turn your fear into a positive thing if you use it to motivate you to action instead of allowing your fears to paralyze you.

People don't usually think of fear as being the opposite of love. Many think that the opposite of love is hate. But, if you think about it as a magnetic force, love makes you move toward something and fear makes you move away from it. You can see how fear and love are opposites.

In fact, fear lies underneath nearly all hateful or angry feelings.

Think about the people you want to hate, or people who make you angry. For instance, let's consider a backstabbing peer. In reality, aren't you afraid somebody may believe them? Or maybe you are afraid they are going to keep you from getting your next raise or promotion. Worse yet, are you afraid they just might be right? These are all natural, underlying fears. In another section, we will delve into more details on fear.

For now, we will identify our two basic core emotions as love and fear, or looked at another way, pleasure or pain. Love brings you pleasure and fear can result in pain.

Primary Emotions

Primary emotions are the next level of emotions. These are the emotions we typically overlook, ignore, or pretend do not exist. To best harness our emotional power, it is vital that we recognize and keep in tune with our primary emotions.

To harness the power of emotions, we must identify the primary emotions. For the greatest control, these emotions should be used to motivate us forward and keeps us out of trouble. Any emotion could be a primary emotion depending upon the situation.

Primary emotions are the ones again that we typically downplay and avoid. We may say, "Oh, it's not a big deal," or "Oh, it doesn't matter," or "Oh, just let it go. Let it go. Let it go."

Don't Skip Primary Emotions

We are prone to over-react when we ignore our primary emotions. It's important to reflect and wait before taking action in order to avoid this escalation. We often regret what we say or do because we have allowed ourselves to go directly to the secondary emotional state. Secondary emotions often display as things like rage or some form of anger, revenge, devastation or being so overwhelmed we will simply give up.

A High-Level Overview of Emotions

Core: The ones that drive us instinctually:
- Love
- Fear

Primary: The ones we dismiss, such as:
- Annoyance
- Hurt
- Disappointment

Secondary: The ones that are more obvious. Those that move us to some kind of action, such as:
- Anger
- Rage
- Excitement

Let's look at a couple of secondary emotions.

Rage Vs. Anger

Rage typically elicits violence, be it a verbal and/or physical attack.

Anger can be linked to a positive motivating impulse or a negative re-action. Anger is a good thing if you use it as a tool and not as a weapon. How so? It is a very powerful tool when you use it to motivate yourself to action. It is a dangerous weapon if you use it to harm yourself or someone else. Your choice must be to harness it and use it as a tool. As a tool, it is a primary emotion, not a secondary one.

A good example of this is Mothers Against Drunk Drivers. Were they angry? YES! They were furious, but they saw their anger and used it in the primary emotional state. Here, instead of waiting until they were so enraged that they couldn't see clearly, they were able to say, "YES, we are angry! What can we do to change this situation so no one else has to feel this anger?"

They took the anger, harnessed it, and came up with a plan: A desired positive outcome. Then, they worked on changing the situation. Thus, they were able to use anger to motivate themselves to action.

Recognizing Your Current Emotional State

It is vital that we become aware of the different states of emotions and where we are within those states, or more to the point, at what stage we feel each emotion. So, how exactly do we identify the emotions that we are having?

The first step is to understand that we all typically experience at least ten emotions at any given moment. The important thing for us to identify is which one is our primary focus, or motivating factor, at this particular moment.

Let's go through a scenario together: Six months ago, your boss came to you in confidence and told you that the company is at a breaking point. They are either going to make it or they are not. If they don't make it, they will have to close the doors and shut down the business. Your boss also tells you they have a project they'd like you to work on. The project is to remain confidential in order to succeed. The success of the company hinges on this project and on your secret involvement in it.

There's nothing like a little pressure to elicit some emotions! You may possibly be feeling overwhelmed, maybe you feel some frustration, maybe fear, maybe there is some, "Wow, hey, I am really trusted!" Or maybe you feel some pride that they believe you can lead the company to success. There are a lot of emotions you could potentially be experiencing consciously or subconsciously.

Now fast forward to today. You've been working on this project for the entire time. You're on salary, so there is no overtime pay. You have all your same duties, plus this extra "secret" responsibility. You want the company to succeed. You want to succeed! You put your heart and soul into getting things for this project done perfectly.

Last month this same boss told you that you were scheduled to give a presentation at the executive board meeting, revealing the findings of your project. That meeting is scheduled for this morning. Yesterday, you were finishing the final touches on the report when you noticed a glaring typo.

If you have ever written a report that had your name on it for the executive board, you know that you do not want any glaring typos. So, last night, you scoured through the report, page by page, word by word and found every mistake that was humanly possible to find. Then you went back to the copy center, stayed up most of the night to copy, collate, and rebind the report.

This morning you came to work early because the boss is always early for the executive board meetings, and you wanted to give her a chance to review your report beforehand. But, today, the boss doesn't come in until about 15 minutes before the meeting. You are sweating bullets. You have your presentation down. You know you are going to do a good job. Even though it's the last minute, you still want to give the executive summary to your boss before the presentation out of courtesy and respect.

As your boss arrives, you run up to her and hand her the report with the executive summary.

Your boss looks at you puzzled and says, "What is this all about?"

"It's the project I've been working on for the last six months."

"Oh!!! Did I forget to tell you? We decided a couple of weeks ago not to proceed with this project."

What emotions you are feeling?

I usually hear things along the lines of rage, anger, and a few other words I will respectively not repeat. You clearly can see some big secondary emotions going on that could very easily lead to a knee-jerk reaction.

Let's start with some of the primary emotions. What are some primary or underlying emotions that you might be feeling? Some may say relief because they don't have to do the presentation. Some say they feel like they were disrespected, unappreciated or taken advantage of. Some are in shock or denial. Some say things like, "You did NOT just do that to me." Some are just tremendously bewildered. You can see where there are a number of possible underlying emotions.

What are the primary emotions versus the secondary emotions? If you reacted to your boss based on instant rage and anger, you would probably say something that you would later regret. Perhaps you would not regret it, but it would get you into some hot water.

On the other hand, if you can say, "I'd like to talk to you about this. Can we talk later on this afternoon?" That gives you some time to focus and think about the primary emotions. Now you can approach it from a different angle.

Don't dwell on the thought, "I am really angry and I'm ready to hurt someone." Instead, look for the basis of your anger. After some consideration of the emotions, you may approach it from an angle of, "I am surprised that I was not given this information when it was given to you. Since it was not, it leads me to believe that my contributions to the company are not valued."

Later, we will talk about assertive scripts you might use. For now, it is vital to identify that you can approach each situation from a different and more productive angle. You are in control of your thoughts and, therefore, you are in control of your emotions. Harnessing your emotional power stems from being able to identify which emotions you are actually having and which ones you choose to focus on.

Practice Before "The Big One" Hits

To identify your thoughts and emotions, you probably do not want to walk around saying, "What am I thinking? What am I thinking? What am I thinking?" Or, "What are my emotions? What are my emotions? What are my emotions?" That will simply drive you crazy.

What you should do, however, is recognize when your emotions begin to rise. If they are positive emotions, ask yourself, "What am I thinking? I want to know because I want to revisit these thoughts again in order to create a continued positive life for myself."

If they are thoughts that make you feel poorly, hopeless or negative, or if they are disturbing thoughts in some way, ask yourself, "What am I thinking? Do I need to refocus on something else or do I need to find a way to motivate myself to action?" Rather than dwelling on the negative, either find a way to resolve what is creating these thoughts and emotions, or choose to focus on something else.

Vincent Van Gogh said, "Let's not forget that the little emotions are the great captains of our lives, and we obey them without realizing it."

Now that we know how to identify the core emotions, let's look at a few of the positive and a few negative emotions.

CHAPTER 3

Anger

As stated in earlier chapters, anger can either be positive or negative.

Aristotle once said, "Anybody can become angry—that is easy, but to be angry with the right person and to the right degree and at the right time and for the right purpose, and in the right way—that is not within everybody's power and is not easy."

Anger can be a benefit or it can be a curse. It is a benefit if you use it as a tool. It is a curse if you use it as a weapon. To use it as a tool you have two choices: Do something about it, or let it go.

Do Something (or not)

Doing something about the situation could be as simple as communicating. It could be gathering more information. It could be soliciting help from someone else, or it could be removing yourself from the situation. To do any one or several of these things would equate to doing something about it.

If you are not willing or able to take any of these steps, then the only real option you have is to let it go. If it is not bothersome enough to take action, why hold onto it? You must let go.

There is an old adage that some would associate with letting go: "Forgive and forget." I, however, am going to tell you that old adage is just plain wrong.

Never Forget

You do want to forgive, but I encourage you not to forget! Forgetting puts you in a position to go through the same situation over again and again and again. What I suggest you do is to forgive and then refocus.

Yes! Forgive and refocus. Let it rest securely in the recesses of your mind so you can draw upon it; use it for a reference and as a reminder. But, don't dwell on it and don't remind the "offender" that you still remember. That is referred to as a grudge. Instead, focus on things that will create a positive environment for you, your thoughts, and those around you.

So again, if something upsets you, do something about it or let it go.

Sadly, instead of taking action or refocusing, many people are tempted to turn to, "A Third Alternative." That is NOT one of our two options!

Pity Party

This is where we revisit what has upset us time and time again. Like a good friend, we just keep going back as if we find comfort with our visits. This constant revisiting is known as wallowing. We've all done it. We have a fight or an argument with someone, and we keep replaying the incident repeatedly in our heads. "I can NOT believe they did that. I should have just said…"

We revisit it. We become our own victim. We not only allow ourselves to become a victim of the event, the persons' comments or actions, but we actually put ourselves in the position of becoming the victim of our very own thoughts—and we do it over, and over, and over again.

I don't know about you, but I really hate being a victim of someone else. And, being a victim of my own doing is inexcusable!

I cannot change what has happened in the past. What I can do is change what is going to happen from this moment forward. And that is where we need to go. If you use anger as a positive tool, you can motivate yourself to action and do something about it.

Truly Angry

There are three ingredients that, when combined simultaneously, form true anger. The first ingredient is to have a strong emotional response. That's called an adrenalin rush. Second, is to put a negative interpretation on an event. And third, is to perceive a threat to yourself or to someone you love or care about.

Let's take a closer look at the three:

Adrenalin Rush: A strong emotional response typically comes as an adrenalin rush; it happens! When it does, you feel this surge of angry feelings coming up from within. This is what allows some people to think it is okay to "lose control." Understand this, there is no such thing as "losing control." That is simply an excuse some people use for not learning how to use their anger positively. Anger is, and should be, a temporary thing. If you have adrenalin rushing all the time, it overflows, and it no longer works properly. It will destroy your physical body and skew your thoughts.

Negative Interpretation: If you allow yourself to put a positive spin on an event, it will not make you angry. The event may still motivate you to do something, but anger will not be a component of your thoughts.

Threatened: If you don't feel that you or someone else is threatened, you may still see an event as negative, but you can say, "Okay, this is a negative thing/event/person. I am so grateful I don't have to wake up in the morning and look in the mirror at the person who is creating this particular negativity."

Did you know that if you "stuff it" or don't deal with your anger constructively, a five-minute anger event will take your body between two and eight hours to recover from?

Seriously. Two to eight hours to get back to a normal state of well-being if you do not deal with anger in a healthy way.

The healthy way to deal with anger is to do something about it or let it go.

Your Anger

Let's look at what events make you angry. Please know this (in fact, take out a pen and write this down in large letters): People cannot make you angry.

Anger is the interpretation you put on a behavior, an event, or an activity. These things can provide the opportunity for you to get "good and angry," and sometimes (in your mind), justifiably so. The fact remains, no one can "make" you angry.

Anger is a decision you make

When is a reactive display of anger appropriate?

It is generally accepted that anger is the response of last resort. Whether it is an individual, a group, or a nation, anger and violence become the crutch most of us turn to when the following happen:

- Communication stops
- Negotiations breakdown

- You run out of time
- You are no longer willing to try
- You stop believing the other person has value
- The desire to have your way outweighs the rights of others
- You feel powerless

Think about this, do you ever remember an appropriate display of anger at work? Most of us can't remember one single incident. When anger in the workplace is displayed, individuals are usually deemed to be out of control, and therefore, no longer trustworthy.

How about in our private lives? Do you remember seeing an angry mother or father disciplining their child in public? Do you remember the revulsion and critical firestorm it created?

This type of anger does not work in the long run. It simply delays resolution of the event. For every angry response, there will be a day to come that you will have to deal with the root of the response.

Triggers

So what makes it okay for you to display anger in this manner? The correct answer here is "nothing."

For each event that causes you to go to anger, look at the event or at the behavior and then ask yourself, "How am I interpreting this? Why do I feel that anger is the most appropriate response?"

Sometimes, all you need is more information. Most times, you have to communicate with yourself as well as with the other person.

Journal the thoughts and feelings you are having. I want you to journal some of the events that have taken place in your world that have led you to a place of anger.

What thoughts provoked your anger?

What other feelings did you have in addition to that anger?

Once you have completed this task, take time to write in your journal how you are going to use that anger to motivate yourself to a specific action next time. What productive actions might you take next time?

Clean Freak

I stuffed anger for many years. My ex-husband knows I tell this story. I did love that man, but the first several years of our marriage set the groundwork for a dysfunctional relationship. I allowed myself to feel like a constant failure due to a lack of two-way communication.

We were both "neat freaks." I was excited when we got married that we would both be "neat freaks" together. We would have a happy, clean home. I did not realize, however, that our standards of neatness were not the same.

You see, his mother spring-cleans every Saturday, and I do mean EVERY Saturday. Growing up we spring-cleaned our home maybe once or twice a year. When we cleaned, we cleaned well. I had a hard time with dirt and disarray, to the point that I could not do anything else until I was happy with the level of "clean" around me.

In the era and the culture when I was raised, it was the married woman's job to keep the house clean, even if both of you worked. I felt like cleaning was my responsibility. I would not succeed as a wife, housekeeper, mother, a woman, and as a human being unless my house was spotless.

Every day, I cleaned that house until it was spotless. And every day, my ex-husband, bless his soul, would come home and re-clean everything behind me.

Personal Interpretations Are Seldom Correct

At first, I was shocked. The house was spotless. He would come home, and, without saying a word, start cleaning.

Then the shock turned to denial. It would say to myself, "Oh, my goodness, what is wrong with me? I must have sold him faulty equipment. I can't clean as well as I thought I could. He has to go behind me and re-clean. I am truly a failure."

So, I would say, "Honey, didn't I do that good enough?"

He would say, "Oh no, it's fine."

"Fine" was a killer word for me. My definition of "fine" was: "You are so worthless that it doesn't even do any good to tell you about it." So I misinterpreted "fine," stuffed it, and I internalized it as failure.

I became anal. I scrubbed that house from top to bottom every single day. I got up in the wee hours of the morning to make sure everything was spotless before we both went to work. I rushed home to make sure everything was still spotless before he got home.

When I vacuumed, my children were not allowed to go into that particular room again until their father got home and saw the vacuum lines on the carpet. They were allowed no more than three toys at a time. They couldn't play with anything else until all three of those toys had been put away.

The cooking utensils used to prepare dinner were washed and put away before we ate. The only things left unwashed were the serving dishes and the plates needed to eat.

I scrubbed my toilets, tubs and sinks every single morning.

Okay, you get the point; I was anal! But, I kept that house spotless!

No matter how hard I worked, he would come home and clean behind me. Each time it happened, I allowed myself to be hurt by it. It only confirmed the extent of my failure.

I was disappointed in myself. I felt disappointed in him. I had a lot of emotions going on. I didn't know what else to do, so I just stewed over the emotions. I let them grow and fester and bubble.

Who Has The Problem?

It took me many years to get good and angry. Then it took a couple more to get to the point that I was willing to use that anger as a tool instead of a weapon.

You see, all those years, I had been using it as a weapon to hurt myself. I was killing myself, physically, on a cellular level, from not using my emotions to help me see there was a problem that I needed to resolve. After all, I was the only one with a problem. Right?

Here's another one you must write down: "If it doesn't bother me, it's not a problem that I have to deal with." And the corollary (write this down too): "If it bothers me, it's my problem and I am responsible for doing something about it or letting it go!"

Christmas Massacre

Several years into the marriage, we moved to a small town to be dorm parents at a community college. We lived in a little, itsy-bitsy, two-bedroom apartment with our three children. In this town, and the surrounding areas, everything closed on Sundays, regardless of what day of the year it was. That year, Christmas Eve fell on a Sunday.

I was excited. This would be the first time in our marriage that he would be able to spend Christmas Eve with the kids and me. Since he worked in retail, he normally had to work long hours every Christmas

Eve. This year he would be home and we were going to have Christmas Eve together at last.

I wanted to make sure everything was perfect for the day, and I certainly did not want to spend it cleaning. This was to be a day of celebration with my family!

I arranged for one of the girls from the dorm who had not gone home for the holidays to take my children for the entire day and most of the night so I could scour that little two-bedroom apartment.

Immediately after he left for work early Saturday morning, I took out my trusty cleaning toothbrush and I scrubbed every crevice and crack that I could imagine or find. I scrubbed the door-frames, the walls, the floorboards, and the tiles; I cleaned at least six inches down the drain of the tub, and cleaned the sinks. I didn't stop until everything sparkled.

I had cleaned the cupboards, behind and under the refrigerator. I soaked and cleaned the refrigerator grill and put it back on the refrigerator as the final task of my cleaning day.

I was in the process of pushing the refrigerator back into place when my husband came home.

I was very pleased with myself! I knew he could, in no way, find a single fault with this place. It was absolutely spotless!

Do you know what he did? He opened the cupboards and began to rearrange the spices!

The Final Straw

That did it! Remember earlier, when I said one of the anger triggers was feeling powerless? It now became clear to me that my best would never be good enough. I was powerless to make this better. Now I lost it!

I let my anger boil up to a point that I finally began to communicate in a way that made it very clear what I thought the problem was. It was perhaps not the clearest or most coherent account of my frustrations, but I let him have it all.

I told him of all the emotions I had been feeling for the previous eight years. I told him the behavior and the events that had created in me the thoughts and the emotions that I was feeling and displaying. I read him chapter and verse of every time I'd cleaned and he'd come behind me and done it again. And it was a very long book!

Do you know what I found out that night? In my anger, after eight years, I finally asked why he followed behind me cleaning. I now know it was exactly the right thing to do. This is Stephen Covey's fifth habit, "seek first to understand then to be understood." It was the right question. It was just eight years late.

For the first time, I asked him, "Why?" Do you know what I discovered?

He didn't clean because it was dirty; he never had.

He cleaned because it was a stress relief for him. He cleaned because it was a way for him to feel in control of his environment. He cleaned so that he could spend time with me and show me how much he loved me.

No, he didn't clean because it was dirty. He never felt like our house was dirty. To him it was always spotless. Oops.

Anger, properly applied (more or less), led us to an understanding that changed the way we looked at our world.

I unknowingly used the pent up anger to motivate myself to action. In this case, the action was to communicate for understanding and resolution. We communicated that night (rather loudly I might add), and we finally came to a resolution. It would be his job to clean the house from that point forward, and it would be my job to help him. Our house was never as spotless again.

The key is to recognize the anger you have, and then use it to motivate yourself to positive action before it starts to attack you and those around you!

Positive action is defined as something that resolves an issue while allowing relationships to grow. Not all actions are positive. This is why you never should allow your anger to speak. The root of your anger is what you talk about, perhaps at length, perhaps loudly, but never angrily. Anger destroys; communication and negotiation uplift.

If you have already wasted years with unresolved anger, do not wait another moment. Anger can and should be a positive influence in your life and your relationships. Now is the time to do something about it!

CHAPTER 4

Additional Emotions Reviewed

L ET US VISIT SOME ADDITIONAL EMOTIONS THAT ARE TYPICAL.

Resentment

I see resentment as a negative. There's an old adage that resentment is like drinking poison and waiting for the other person to die. It is not going to have any effect on the other person. However, it will have a devastating effect on you and all of your relationships. It will kill you, slowly and painfully.

I'm not saying that it will kill you metaphorically. Resentment will LITERALLY kill you. There have been studies that show a strong correlation between emotional resentment and heart disease. So YES! Resentment can literally kill you.

You may resent a situation. You may wish you hadn't done something or that something had not happened to you. You have the same choices that you had with anger, either do something about it or let it go.

Situations you revisit with resentment will build to a deeper resentment. The emotion of resentment has both a negative mental and physical effect.

Joy

Joy, of course, is positive. There's a saying, "Every day may not be a good day, but there is something good in every day." I like that quote.

My mother would say, "Remember, it will all be all right in the end. If it's not all right, it's not the end." That is a nice way to look at things as well.

When you have joy, things around you seem to fall into place and everything seems to work out just fine. To keep that happening, you have to maintain an overriding sense of joy.

The key to joy is two-fold. First, be grateful. Be grateful for the little things, the big things, and the ones in between. Then find those things, events, and thoughts that bring you the greatest joy, and focus on them. Build your life around joyful events even while understanding that not all will be joyous. You will find, as many others have, that more joy exists if that is where your focus lies. Later, we will talk more about joy and gratitude as we talk about attitudes.

Enthusiasm

Enthusiasm is simply to delight and be engaged in the experiences around you. Be engaged, create, and help to find joy. Create a sense of happy urgency that permeates your life and flows to others.

Fear

We've already talked a bit about fear. We said that fear can be negative or positive. It is positive if it moves you forward; not so positive if it paralyzes you. Of course, you do need a healthy fear response to know when you are in a potentially dangerous situation. Without fear, you could really get yourself in trouble. Some fear is healthy, but living in fear is not.

I like the acronym of F.E.A.R., "False Evidence Appearing Real." If it is real, it is a fact. If it is false evidence that appears real, you must figure out why you would think it is real. Get more information. Figure out if this is something coming from within you or if it is something about the situation you are in.

Why does it cause you to fear?

You will need to deal with two types of fear. The first, I'll call fear #1, is an immediate, "I'm in danger now!" type of fear. It is almost always best to heed this type of fear, and do something to remove yourself from the situation. Later you can worry about how you got there, and how you should deal with future situations like that.

The other, I'll call fear #2, is one that you see coming. It's something that you plan, that your friends plan for you, or that you have committed to doing such as: Bungee jumping, rock climbing, public speaking, stand-up comedy, blind dating… The list is endless. You have the ability to fear anything. You also have the ability to choose not to be afraid.

First, determine if it is something to truly fear. Then figure out what you can do to move beyond it. Fear has uncertainty at its core. That is why it exists. For you, there is something unknown in your fear. Thus, if you can transform what you fear to something certain, then it moves from a core fear to an actual fact. And facts, no matter how heinous or distasteful, are much easier to deal with than an uncertain fear is.

Again, I want to take a moment and clarify that some fear is healthy and actually is a key factor in our safety. The fear #1 that I talked about is the fear of imminent harm that keeps us from treading into dangerous situations unnecessarily, or alerts us when we do. Pay attention to that.

No. 1 vs. No. 2

But the question then becomes, "Where is the dividing line?" and "What is a healthy versus an unhealthy dose of fear?" or perhaps, "What can I do about irrational fear?"

Here is an example of irrational fear that could be termed unhealthy. I had an unhealthy dose of fear when it came to spiders. "Ew!" I know you may have just got the creepy crawlies.

That is how I felt 20 years ago.

If you had told me I had to choose between being thrown into a pit of King Cobras or a pit of Daddy Long Legs, even though I know Daddy Long Legs fangs are not big enough to bite me, I would have gladly chosen the pit of Cobras.

I would rather have died of venom than of fear.

Years ago, when I managed a State Parks and Recreations call center, I was asked to visit each campground to gather information about the various campsites to share with the public.

As I started traveling and camping at these campgrounds, I realized I had to overcome my fear of spiders. A lot of these campgrounds had a lot of spiders. Though I had always been terrified of spiders, with some research I found most spiders were harmless. I also learned that there are some spiders you should treat with healthy respect. Some are dangerous and some can be deadly.

I had to find out what a Hobo spider looked like, how poisonous it was, and the regions where I would be most likely to encounter one. What did a common garden spider look like? What kind of harm can it really cause, or not?

As I continued to research the various nuances of spiders, I began to appreciate the beauty and intricacies of the webs that they weave, the lives they live, and the dangers they present. Slowly, my overwhelming fear of spiders began to dissolve. It wasn't that I was no longer afraid, but I now realized that I'd lumped all spiders in to my phobia because I simply didn't know what might actually hurt me. And after all, isn't most fear based, at its core, on the premise that you are going to be hurt?

I still have a healthy dose of fear of certain types of spiders in certain regions, but I also know where and when to keep a careful watch for them and what to do to prevent them from biting me. I know how to protect myself from those spiders.

Spiders are still not allowed to live in my home. If I feel the need to kill one or to move one outside, I can do it myself. I no longer run from a room screaming or crying for someone else to come take care of it.

The fear, instead of paralyzing me, helps to motivate me to action.

So in this scenario, what is fact versus false evidence?

Facts: Certain spiders are dangerous. Most are not.

False Evidence Appearing Real: All spiders want to kill me, and could eat me alive in a single bite.

Love

I see love as very positive. Notice that I said love not lust. Lust is not a positive emotion. Lust runs more along the lines of jealousy. It is a purely physical attraction and has no lasting effect. It contains the thought, "I must have something someone else has."

Love, on the other hand, is pure and selfless. Many times, it has nothing to do with sex. In addition, regardless of the source, it brings you an overwhelming sense of joy and turns your focus from yourself to the object of your love. Have you ever noticed that when you're in love, everything seems to run more smoothly? Everything seems happier and more blissful around you. There have been countless novels and movies on how a person's life changes when they finally find true love.

Love Changes You

If you look at the events in a person's life, you will realize that most things have not changed. What has changed is the way the person acts and reacts to events. These actions and reactions will lead to other actions and reactions. People who get glimpses of love do things like pay it forward, leave a large tip, or help someone else (usually anonymously).

This is an extremely important point, so I want you to highlight it and repeat the phrase clearly:

"The reason your life changes when you find love has NOTHING TO DO WITH THE OTHER PERSON."

YOU changed. The way you act and react, the way you frame the world in your thoughts and the way you choose to interpret events changes when you fall in love. When you change, your life changes.

What is Love?

What are the key elements of love? We typically think of love as one person's devotion for another. Though this is true, it is only one of several key elements. Another key element requires that you know yourself. As you do, you choose to fully accept, love, respect, and honor yourself. You can only love others to the extent that you love yourself.

This is a key element that many miss. To truly love another, you must love yourself, and understand and do those things that bring you to your highest level of joy and satisfaction. You must continually meet your own social and emotional needs.

The only way to do that with lasting effect, and this sounds counterintuitive, is to turn your focus away from yourself. Learn to make it possible for others to experience joy. As you do, they realize the person helping them is worthy of their love.

While you first must be your own friend, it is extremely important that you find and develop friendships, be a friend to others, and create a value for yourself in other people's eyes.

In short, serve others. Take time to connect with people, because sharing and service is where it all starts. You cannot love something you don't know. Allowing others to know you, allows you to be loved.

So, the goal of love is to use those things that bring you to your highest level of joy and satisfaction, and find or create friends with whom you can share your passion. That is love.

Anxiety

Anxiety is another tough one. Anxiety again can be either positive or negative. To quote Rolo May, "As long as it is not out of proportion to a situation, anxiety is good for you."

There is a close relationship between anxiety and creativity, originality and intelligence. A healthy dose of anxiety will move you forward. Without anxiety, you are not likely to go anywhere. Anxiety in this sense is uneasiness with the status quo. It's the thing that generates urgency. It represents a discomfort that creates a need for change or improvement. Anxiety can be something that moves you forward, or like fear, something that paralyzes you.

In fact, many times the two words are used to describe exactly the same circumstances. Anxiety is the manifestation of fear. Fear, over a short time, creates anxiety. Like fear, the choices are the same: act now, create a plan to deal with it, or dismiss it.

Disappointment

Another primary emotion is disappointment. Disappointments are unrealized expectations. In short, you had an expectation and things did not unfold the way you wanted them to.

People deal with disappointment every day. Damage from disappointment is dependent upon how big the disappointment is and how you choose to deal with it. Think of pessimists and optimists.

For many, unresolved disappointment elicits a sense of hopelessness and leads to depression and apathy, which then leads to paralysis. This chain reaction is often far more painful to experience than anger or rage.

An unresolved disappointment often settles into an unhealthy apathy about life in general and leads to an abyss that is difficult to escape. This is when a person begins to believe nothing will ever work out. They simply accept that their expectations will not be met and do nothing to improve their situation.

To this I say, if your expectations are not being met, and you want to avoid disappointment, simply change your expectations.

You have no control over the actions of others. More to the point, you should not expect to have that control. Most disappointment stems from unrealized expectations you have for someone else. When that is true, you have already made a mistake.

You have to acknowledge that on most occasions, someone will not behave according to your expectations. This is especially true when you don't actually tell them what you expect. Likewise, if you know someone will not laugh at your jokes, stop expecting them to.

Learn to stop projecting your needs on others. Drop your expectations and work with those you care about who share a common goal. But, only expect those things that you both agree on. And when you can't agree, do not create expectations.

If you need someone to laugh with and you can't do that with present company, find someone else to laugh with. If you "expect" something from someone, find someone who can provide it.

Self-Acceptance

This all leads to the next primary emotion. In my opinion, self-acceptance is one the most important.

Though we all make choices we wish we had not, we are the people we are today because of them. You have done it perfectly at this point. Every decision, every action, every thought, everything you do, and everything you are, has led you to this point. Had you not made all those things happen, you would not be reading this book right now, you would not be the person you are.

It is critical that you understand that positive self-acceptance is a vital emotion. You have done everything perfectly to come to this point in your life. Accept that you have. Cherish it, and accept yourself for having come to this point. Encourage yourself and your loved ones to experience the beauty and peace of self-acceptance as often as possible. Self-acceptance is the act of being loving and happy with the person you are now. It is an agreement with yourself to appreciate, validate, accept, and support who you are at this moment. And, after reflection, you may also feel a sense of urgency about some items in your life that could use improvement.

Comparative Emotions

Pessimism vs. Optimism

According to Southern Kings Consolidated School, pessimism and optimism are simply a choice in how you view things.

Have you ever wondered why some people feel down and defeated when faced with difficult situations, while others feel challenged and hopeful? Or why some people get all worked up and angry over small inconveniences and disagreements, while others respond more positively? These opposite emotions and reactions are due to how people interpret events—whether they view things from an optimistic or a pessimistic point of view.

The defining characteristic of people with pessimistic feelings is that they tend to believe hardships will happen to them and last a long time, undermining everything that they do, and they are the root of the problem. It is their fault.

On the other hand, people with optimistic feelings, when confronted with the same situations, believe that defeat is a temporary setback; its causes are confined to that one situation. They are not at fault.

The difference between optimistic and pessimistic feelings isn't a difference in life experiences, but rather in how you perceive and respond to adversity. When going through hardships, an optimist assumes life will get better. A pessimist believes life will always be difficult and possibly more painful.

A pessimist will latch onto "the real world" argument. They will fault the optimist for being completely unrealistic.

An optimist will feel sorry for the pessimist, knowing the world is not a dark and gloomy place.

Achieving a balance of realism and hope can be a challenge. We see that people with optimistic feelings will try harder to change a difficult situation. While the outcomes of both approaches might be similar, the road to that outcome can take a great toll on the pessimist.

Studies have shown that these different approaches to life affect our health. Optimists generally have better health, age better (and less), and experience fewer physical problems associated with aging.

Envy vs. Jealousy

I see envy as potentially positive and jealousy as negative with no upside.

Here is the Dr. Karen definition of the two:

Envy: You have something really cool and I would like something like it, so, I am going to work hard to obtain something similar. You still get to keep what you have, and I want something like it for myself.

Jealousy: You have something cool. It's not fair. You don't deserve it. So I am going to take it away from you, make it very difficult for you to keep it, or I am going to one-up you in a way that makes it obvious that I'm better and deserve more.

Everybody deserves what they have. And if they really don't deserve it, trust me, Karma (fate) will take care of them.

Here's one for the high school boys (and sometimes girls). Have you ever heard of a case where one boy decides that he is going to fight another boy for his girlfriend? The justification, he believes, is that whoever wins the fight, wins the girl. Whether you know it or not, this is simple jealousy. The boy who wants to fight, doesn't understand the rules of life and is not willing to do the work required to help the girl understand that he is the better choice. He believes that merely using violence and defeating his opponent gives him the right to the girl. This is wrong on so many levels.

Yet many adults operate in this mode most of their lives. "Survival of the fittest" is a civilization destroyer. It only works in an animal kingdom where there are no rules of society or civilization. Never forget that.

Where does fairness come into the question? Simple, life is not fair. Appealing to the laws of fairness only pushes you into an impossible environment of negative rage, resentment, unfairness, and anger that will eat you alive.

Jealousy is toxic! There is no excuse for it. Jealousy is an indication of a lack of moral conviction, a desire not to work for the things you want, and a solid step in the direction of insanity. Avoid jealousy at all costs!

Empathy Vs. Pity

We will discuss empathy specifically as one of our key components later. For now, simply put, empathy is positive. It's where you feel with somebody. Pity is where you look down upon someone and feel sorry for them. I don't want anyone to pity me; I want them to feel with me, and allow me the freedom to feel as well.

You are Building a Person

Think of self-acceptance as being okay with the house you live in right now. This does not mean it is the only house you will ever have, or that it's exactly the way you want it. One day you might want to add a room, create a nicer house, or change the style of the house. You might sell it and buy a newer one.

It is great to work towards creating and living in your dream house, but in the meantime, look for and appreciate the advantages to the home where you live. You can be happy with the house you have now even as you build towards that dream of your bigger house. One day it will become a reality. This does not mean you settle. It means you love the person you are while working towards being the person you want to be.

Self-acceptance also leads to a life with new possibilities. Love and self-acceptance keep you from being caught up in the struggle against what you perceive as reality.

Some people have trouble accepting themselves because of their lack of motivation. Others have the misconception that if you are satisfied with yourself, you are unlikely to change or improve.

These don't have to be true. You don't have to be unhappy with yourself to identify, acknowledge and actively work on changing character flaws. Self-acceptance is the first step in change.

Self Evaluation

There may be hundreds of emotions for you personally. They all lead to a variety of places. To begin your transformation, acknowledge and evaluate the emotions that are creating our own personal reality today.

You can relate to what I'm saying if you've ever heard the comment, "They live in their own little world." Every one of us lives in our own world. We have a set of realities that is unique to us. Some of us have a lot of realities in common with others. Some of us have only a few. Being "normal" can be a curse or a bonus. Most inventive people aren't what you would consider normal. The fact remains that you have some portion of your reality that works well for you. You also have some that could really use some work.

In these chapters, I've shared some of my own experiences, emotional trials, and some personal struggles I went through while learning how to harness my emotional power. I'm far from done, and there is value in what I have learned.

Now it is your turn. Take time to reflect on your own experiences. Identify your key, driving emotions so you can begin your own path to harnessing your emotional power.

Points to Ponder

Here are a few additional emotions for your evaluation. You may come up with some additional ones of your own. At some point, when you can take the time to really ponder it, look at the list that's been provided as well as your own. Put a check mark by the emotions you see as a positive influence in your life and cross-out the ones that you see as negative. Some could be crossed-out and have a check-mark because they could be either.

Write down and evaluate the ones that you find yourself typically feeling, and the impact they have on your life.

Check the emotions that are positive and cross out the ones that are negative:

 Annoyance
 Frustration
 Rage
 Guilt
 Shame
 Happiness
 Sadness

List others for you to ponder. You may experience these often:

_____

_____

_____

_____

_____

_____

_____

_____

_____

_____

Let's do a quick peek into your mind. I want you to think about something you did this morning. Using just a few key words, write down what you did.

_____

_____

_____

_____

_____

_____

Now without stopping to think, write down ten emotions you are having this very moment.

1.

2.

3.

4.

5.

6.

7.

8.

9.

10.

You may be stuck on one emotion, or maybe you got two or three. Most people are going, "UHHH, UHHH..." and have a hard time listing any.

We all feel at least ten emotions at any given moment. However, we have to become aware of the emotions we're having. This allows us to use them to our advantage, to move ourselves forward and put our emotions to work on our behalf.

This list you just created is the skeletal base for harnessing your own personal emotional power. Recognizing the emotions that you are experiencing and deciding which ones are necessary to work on (or with) is where you will find peace and where you will find power. Take a minute to finish that list. If you can't get ten, strive for a minimum of six.

John Sterling says, "Emotion turning back on itself, and not leading on to thought or action, is the element of madness."

Don't put yourself into madness. Put yourself in the position of moving forward and leading yourself to action.

We have covered a lot in the last few chapters! We have covered many of the emotions that we feel in our lives. We have shared some stories and learned by example.

In the next chapter, we are going to talk about the concept of emotional space and how you can best use it.

CHAPTER 5

Emotional Space

THE LAST ELEMENT OF AWARENESS WE ARE GOING TO DISCUSS comes down to how you use your emotional space.

I like the way my colleague and friend, Joann Corley, explains the term "emotional space." On one side of your emotional space, you have the emotions themselves. On the other side of the space is the outcome, result or action you are looking for. Smack dab in the middle is where your own emotional space resides. In that emotional space, you must recognize the emotion you are having. Acknowledge that you are having the emotion rather than pretending it is not there. Finally, you must allow yourself to feel it fully.

Emotion	Emotional Space (Deal With Emotion)	Outcome Result Action
	• Recognize • Acknowledge • Feel it fully • Process • Diffuse	

Figure 1: Emotional Space Worksheet

First, recognize it; second, acknowledge it; third, feel it fully. Feeling it fully is the most vital step. Without taking this step, you cannot move forward.

You might be saying, "But I don't want to feel angry, but I don't want to feel sad." But, you must feel it. You are entitled to it. You deserve it. Feel it fully. That does not mean that you have the right to wallow in it. It doesn't mean you should get stuck in it. It means you recognize it and you allow yourself to feel it.

You must exercise those emotional muscles in order to open up the brain to possibilities.

Once you have truly felt the emotions, and only after you have done this, can you move to the fourth step, which is to process the emotion, the thought, the event, and the comments.

When you have processed the elements of the emotion, you are now in a position to do the fifth and final step: Use or diffuse the emotions.

Diffusing it does not mean you make it go away; it means you act upon it to move yourself forward. Remember: Do something about it or let it go. You decide the proper course of action for you. Act instead of reacting. When you act, you do things intentionally. When you react, you act impulsively first and then think. In most all cases, you regret that impulse later.

Satisfaction—Can You Get It?

On a positive side of the scale, let's look at something as simple as a basic satisfaction. I get a sense of satisfaction when my current husband enjoys one of my home-cooked meals. It is not something I have the opportunity to do for him often because of our chosen careers. In truth, it was something I didn't realize would make me happy. Because of my travels, I am accustomed to eating out nearly every day.

So when I first noticed I felt this positive feeling I had to:

1. **RECOGNIZE** it. What feeling am I having?
2. **ACKNOWLEDGE** that I feel a sense of accomplishment and a sense of pure satisfaction. Satisfaction is a basic need I have.
3. **FEEL** the warm glow inside that comes from being satisfied with one's behavior.
4. **PROCESS** what it is that makes me feel satisfied. Is it the belief that I've pleased him? Is it the belief that I accomplished a task

or feat (for me cooking can be a major feat)? Perhaps it is that I feel appreciated and I deserve it. Or is it all of the above? By the way, that's the correct answer.

5. **USE instead of DIFFUSE.** In this case, I DO NOT want to change it. I want to duplicate it and revisit it.

Simple enough! Yes, but even though it is simple, it will take some practice!

Look again at the five steps for identifying and maintaining balanced emotional space. I like to call them RAFPU:

Recognize
Acknowledge
Feel it Fully
Process
Use or Diffuse

Practice Makes Permanent

Consider using these five steps now. Write down an emotion you may be concerned with or something you are feeling at the moment.

Go through the five steps of your emotional space and determine what outcome you are actually looking for. Understand that you can work the sequence backwards as well. Sometimes it is easier to start with the outcome and then work with the five steps in the emotional space to identify the specific emotion(s) that allowed the outcome to emerge.

Regardless of how you start, or end, it is vital that you do actively start manage your emotional space.

When you don't, you will get hung up and get yourself in trouble every single time.

Pay Attention

Awareness is the first step in dealing with your emotions. You can choose to allow intense feelings to hijack you and deal with the destruction, or you can choose to channel them into something constructive.

CHAPTER 6

Attitude

A WARENESS IS THE FIRST COMPONENT TO EMOTIONAL POWER. THE second component to emotional power is attitude. It is your responsibility to generate a good attitude at every turn.

Winston Churchill once said, "Attitude is a little thing that makes a big difference."

Life is not always roses and sunshine. Bad things do happen to good people—all the time! The major difference between a life of happiness and a life of misery is having a good attitude and the hope or faith that things will eventually turn out okay.

I like to think of a good attitude as the light at the end of the tunnel. And yes, there is always a light at the end of the tunnel. But it is much more than just seeing the light. These are the times when all feels lost and, even though you faithfully search for that light, you may not be able to see it right now.

Have you had one of those awful days? It's a day when the only attitude you can muster is a bad attitude. Or when someone who cannot possibly understand what you are going through, says to you, "Don't worry there is always a light at the end of the tunnel." Doesn't hearing that just make you want to scream? If your first thought is, "If there is a light, it's probably a train heading straight at me!" then it is time to acknowledge you need to change your attitude. If you don't, you will be stuck in a dark place forever.

You Create Your Attitude

So, how do you keep a good attitude?

To start with, you must keep in mind that there really is always a light at the end of the tunnel.

Now sometimes you may not even be able to see the tunnel around you. Perhaps you cannot see the tunnel because the light is too dim to see entirely. Perhaps it's been dark for so long that you don't realize you are in a tunnel.

A good attitude means holding on until the light begins to brighten, and then having the courage to force yourself forward until you find the exit.

Sometimes as you move through your tunnel, you stumble into an open area that is lined with nooks or caves. You may feel lost in here and question your choices. In these times, it is possible that your tunnel is not directly in front of you. Perhaps you have to reorient yourself and find which direction is right for you. If there is one thing I am certain of, it is that if you diligently look, you will find the rest of the tunnel, and there is always a light at the end of it.

Recognize Where You Are

It is important, however, to recognize that there is a difference between a tunnel and a nook or a cave. Nooks are easy. They are just small indents in the wall that are easy to identify. as we get close. Caves are a little harder. They may be larger, but unlike the tunnel, the hope for light is false. With caves, there is only one way out, and it is the same way you came in. A tunnel, however, always has two openings.

A good attitude in caves is allowing yourself to acknowledge that you've gone into a cave. You just need to figure out how to turn around or simply back out. Sadly, some may find themselves in a cave with no hope of light, but since they are at least out of the storm, they are willing to curl up in a ball and remain in this dark place. Please see your caves for what they are; they are traps. Don't give up your search for a better place.

An example of a cave may be that you feel hopeless because you are in bad relationship. You may fear that no one else would ever want to be with you. Or maybe your true fear is being alone. Because of fear or hopelessness, you remain a prisoner (of your own doing) in that relationship.

If you treat this same example as a tunnel, you would have faith and courage to remove yourself from a bad situation. You recognize there will be a period of darkness and it may be tough for a while. Still, in the end, you will definitely be healthier and will find a more satisfying relationship.

The key is to always look for the light at the end of the tunnel. Remember, tunnels have two openings. You go in one end, and if you keep moving forward, at some point, you will come out on the other side. A good attitude helps you have an open mind so you may recognize the right way through your tunnel. A good attitude gives you the hope and faith to hold on. It gives you the courage to proceed and the strength to step out into the fresh air and light waiting for you at the other end.

What Are You Really Afraid Of?

For some, it is not the awful storm, the dark tunnel or the cave. Their problem is they will not allow themselves to experience happiness when it comes to them. The idea of having happiness is their biggest fear. They have become satisfied with a life in which they are victims regardless of what they do, and where they have learned to expect that their efforts will fail. Because of that, they only go through the motions, but never truly get involved in their own life.

And, because of that complacency, they now believe that a mindset change that requires them to gather or rely on a positive attitude would threaten their very existence. Everything in their life would most likely change. That single thought is almost enough to justify no change at all. The fear is false, but appears real to them.

Your View of the "Real" World

> "Happiness is an attitude. We can either make ourselves miserable, or make ourselves happy and strong. The amount of work is the same."
>
> – Fransisca Riggler

This quote says that it takes the same amount of work to be miserable as it does to be happy. So why would you allow yourself to be miserable? The attitude you choose is truly your option.

Victor Frankl, a renowned doctor and holocaust survivor, explained that the search for happiness will always fail. He stated that happiness is a byproduct of doing things that create a better you. Happiness comes as a result of positive actions and activities. You then have the right to accept happiness or to reject it.

Does that mean you must have a good attitude all the time? Honestly, you most likely won't. There are going to be days when you just do not have a good attitude. But on these days, it is more important than ever to keep the hope, faith, and the desire to have a good attitude again and become happy.

Do you remember the pessimist and the optimist? They are faced with the same opportunities and challenges, yet they have two separate approaches and two different rewards when it's over.

Gratitude is the Key

Learn to be an optimist. The best way I have found to do this is to keep a gratitude journal to remind yourself that things can and will be good, if you allow them to be.

A gratitude journal is a notebook in which you write about your most precious gifts. Every day write down in this journal ten things for which you are grateful.

Maybe someone smiled, held the door open for you or picked up a package that you dropped on the ground. It could be something nice you said to someone or that somebody else said to you. It could be that you are grateful that you live close to the grocery store so you could easily pick up milk on the way home. At the beginning, you may have to pretend to be grateful. Start with the small things: You woke up today. That's a good thing. Your heart is beating, you are breathing, the sun is shining (or not)… Whatever it is, whatever you feel grateful for, write it down.

Note that I gave you an out, "Pretend to be grateful." One of the strongest agents for change is the desire to change. That is coupled with practice. Practice long enough and it becomes a habit. Practice long enough and you believe in yourself. Practice long enough and what you practice becomes a part of you. So, practice being grateful.

The Not-So-Grateful Me

This was a challenge for me. When I first started my gratitude journal many years ago, I couldn't think of a single thing to be grateful for. That first day I said, "Okay I am grateful that...um... Well... ummm..." I couldn't think of anything.

Finally, my husband said, "Can you breathe?"

I said, "Well, yeah."

He said, "Well, aren't you grateful you can breathe?"

Quite honestly, at that moment, I was not so sure if I was or not. I was definitely caught in the "not-good attitude" lifestyle.

Sadly, during those first two weeks, all I could do was write down bodily functions, because I could not think of anything else to be grateful for. Today I have to limit myself to just ten things. I can come up with a whole gamut of things to be grateful for on any given day, and really, at any given moment.

It is truly amazing. The more I am grateful, the more things I find to be grateful for. And the more grateful I am, the more positive things happen for me, around me, to me, and with me. Not that long ago, my grandson told me I was his Cinderella princess. Awww, isn't that a great thing to be grateful for? Doesn't that just make your heart feel good? It's sweet, so of course it does. Right?

To be truthful, I didn't have such a good attitude when my children were that young. If one of my children at the age of four had said "Mommy you are my Cinderella princess," I would have said, "What do you want?" or "Okay, what did you do?" But now I hear it and my heart says "Oh, he loves me!"

It's All About You

You know, it is all about changing your perception. Your attitude changes your perception. Your attitude is what opens or closes your mind to the possibilities of a better life.

A good attitude is an understanding that there is a light at the end of the tunnel, even if the outline of the tunnel is not always clear. A good attitude is having hope and a personal faith in yourself, in your capabilities, and in the knowledge that, "It will be alright, or maybe even fantastic."

It is allowing yourself to have something to hold onto. You believe in the basic goodness of life, and in a higher power. That power can be the laws of the universe, the laws of the land, the laws of attraction, karma, fate or any religious beliefs you may choose to embrace. Have faith that there is always something to believe in and to hope for—something that will change your life for the better.

That is having a good attitude.

So, get started now. Take five minutes and create the first page in your journal. Write a date on it, then fill it out. All ten, no slacking!

Gratitude Journal

Today I am grateful for:

1. _____

2. _____

3. _____

4. _____

5. _____

6. _____

7. _____

8. _____

9. _____

10. _____

CHAPTER 7

Empathy

L ET'S GET EMPATHIC! EMPATHY GOES HAND-IN-HAND WITH ATTITUDE.

The Merriam Webster definition of empathy is :

The action of understanding, being aware of, being sensitive to and vicariously experiencing the feelings, thoughts and experiences of another of either the past or present without having the feelings, thoughts or experiences fully communicated in an objectively explicit manner.

Okay, that is a great definition. I like to look at it in a little bit simpler way. Dr. Karen's definition is:

Empathy is removing yourself as the focal point and understanding the other persons' point of view, needs and emotions.

Empathy presupposes the understanding that while you have a right to your thoughts and emotions, the expression of those must be appropriate for the situation. Your right to "act out" does not extend to degrading another person. Poor behavior is always unacceptable. Empathy is also accepting that others also have a right to their thoughts and emotions but not necessarily the right to improper behaviors. Finally, empathy is a learned behavior that allows you to set aside your pride and self-image so that you can feel and understand how someone else may be feeling.

The terms "Put yourself in their shoes," "Walk a mile in their shoes," "Feel what they feel," and even, "Do unto others as they would have you do unto them" (The Platinum Rule), are all examples of wise people urging us to learn and use empathy in our lives.

It's All About Them

What are some ways you can have empathy? One way is to allow yourself to feel fully. That goes back to the emotional space we discussed earlier. Empathy is also the ability to allow others to feel fully.

Obviously, never encourage or allow others to do something physically or emotionally harmful. Remember that when their behavior is not necessarily appropriate or good it must be addressed. But to personally have and to show empathy you must allow the other person to feel and to express their feelings. The other major aspect of empathy again is to remove yourself as a focal point and allow the other person to become the focal point and express their fears and concerns.

Selfish?

A few years ago, I was holding my own self-serving, pity-party day. I say self-serving because pity-parties are just that. They are a form of selfishness that is foreign to gratitude and deny you from accessing any form of empathy.

On this day, I had chosen to feel sorry for myself. Yes, it is a choice. I am going to say that again so that you may choose to hear it: It is a choice! I had chosen the opposite of gratitude. I was having one of those days when you are irritable from the time you get up. Everything around you is annoying and you just feel like being irritable. You don't want anybody telling you not to be irritable, and you certainly don't want to think about gratitude.

That day, I told myself, "You know what? Quite frankly today is a bad day and I just don't want to be happy. I want to enjoy the musings of my bad day."

On this particular day, I was allowing myself one of these miserable days. I don't have them very often, but man, I was having one then.

Bad, Then Worse

Here is the story: I was speaking in my hometown, which normally is a great thing. But this day it was irritating to me because my family was going to be away from home that evening. After my seminar I had five whole hours to sit at the airport, in my own hometown, before my plane took off.

I could have gone home, but then I'd just be sitting at home doing nothing as well. On top of that, I would have to either pay for airport parking or for a cab to take me to the airport. So, I figured that I might as well go to the airport on the hotel shuttle where I was presenting that day. At least then, I would have a slight chance of catching an earlier flight. That is, if there was one and it was not overbooked already.

Wow, even I can hear how irritable and negative I was being. I was also irritable because my flight was so late in the evening that it meant I would not get to the next city until the wee hours of the next morning.

That morning, everything seemed to go haywire. Setting up the room, everything went wrong. There were not enough tables or chairs. The people who were supposed to assist me didn't show up on time. The hotel couldn't find the boxes with the meeting materials. I mean, come on, nothing was going right. Everything that could go wrong, did go wrong.

Since I teach and preach about having a good attitude, I was doing my best not to show how grumpy and irritable I was. I was trying to pretend I was having a good day, But I was not having a good day! I was having a BAD, BAD day. And, I was having a pity party instead of displaying empathy.

I was feeling sorry for myself. I could have said, "I am entitled to have feelings," and allowed myself to feel and process these emotions. Or, I could have shelved them and processed them later at a more appropriate time. Instead of empathy, I was wallowing in a "woe is me" day. I knew that I had the option of feeling it and moving on by saying, "Okay, this is not my ideal day." Instead, I made my negativity and my feelings the focal point of everything around me.

The day seemed to drag on and on forever. About 15 minutes before the end of my speaking engagement, someone from the hotel came rushing into the room and said, "We have an emergency call for you."

Now most of you just thought, "Oh no, what happened?" The sad truth is, I was in such a foul mood, having such a wonderful pity-party for myself, that my thought was not, "Oh no, something bad may have happened." Instead it was, "Somebody better be dead or dying, or I am going to kill them for interrupting my session."

I now regret that hideous, horrible, and self-centered thought. To this day the negativity that I spewed out at that moment still haunts me.

Fortunately, no one died. But the emergency was equally as heart-breaking. You see, on that day, my youngest son attempted suicide and was being rushed to the Emergency Room.

Turn Outside of Yourself

Now, this was such shocking news that my ingrained habits kicked in. From 16 years of practicing nearly every day, the task of coming up with and writing down ten gratitudes, my survival instincts kicked in, and I turned to an attitude of gratitude. My shocked mind, in a state of not knowing what else to do, instantly went there out of shear habit.

So, why didn't my mind go there when I was just irritable? Because I was not allowing myself to feel why I was so irritated. I was just having pity for myself. I had made a choice to wallow. I wasn't having any part of empathy for myself, or for the other people around me.

Whenever I tell this story, someone always asks this question, "What did you have to be grateful for at that moment?" Honestly, not a whole lot. Yet, as my gratitude kicked in, I started to realize I could be grateful for many things.

Gratitudes:
1. He was not successful at the suicide attempt.
2. He had been found and was being rushed to ER.
3. We had a leading hospital in the area that deals with this type of situation.
4. I am in my hometown and I have five hours I can spend in ER with him.
5. I have a best friend who has gone through a similar situation.
6. I am not grateful she has gone through the situation but that I had the opportunity to learn with her what to expect.
7. I am grateful that I have a best friend that I can call and cry with.
8. I am grateful for my friends and family, and for the love and support I know they are going to give my son and me.
9. I am grateful for my faith.
10. I am grateful that I can learn from this experience.
11. I am grateful.

Okay, you have to admit, there were many things to be grateful for that day, but what if he had not, survived? What if he had been successful with his attempt? I believe my gratitudes from years of habit would still have kicked in. They might not have been as positive, or as many, but still they would have been there. Here are some that could have been:

- I am grateful he is not in pain any longer.
- I am grateful that I have a best friend I can call and cry with.
- I am grateful for family, for the love and support I know they are going to give me.
- I am grateful, I am grateful, I am grateful.

See, these gratitudes removed ME from the focal point of, "Oh, woe is me!" They helped me move past the anger at myself, and the guilt for not knowing or realizing his pain. It allowed me to love and forgive myself for not knowing what was happening in his mind and heart that had brought him to this point.

It took me out of that place of anger and pity into a place of focusing on the real situation at hand, to the real person that needed me to focus on them. It helped me focus on my son and what he must be going through.

Effective Empathy

That attitude of gratitude and that empathy put me in a position of emotional power I didn't know I had. Nor did I realize how much I was displaying it until months later. I did not know until Mother's Day about nine months after the event, when my wonderful son, who was now healthy and happy, wrote an ode to Mother.

What he explained was that it was my ability to focus on him and what he must be going through, and my ability to have empathy for him that gave him the strength to hold on and carry forward after descending into the aftermath of his darkest hour. It was my ability to use my emotional power.

He didn't have to coddle me, apologize to me, worry about how I was reacting, or how I might react next. He didn't have to worry about how I was feeling and what I was going to think, or how I was going to judge him. Knowing that gave him the strength to take care of himself. It was my ability to see that things could be okay that opened my mind to the possibility and allowed me to use the tools that I had to help him.

There is one tool I had used for myself for years, yet sadly, I suddenly realized I had never used with him. If I had, we may not have had the conversation we did that night. That night while in the ER, we discussed this tool of hope. I told him, "Every night for the next two weeks, I am going to call you." Because I knew that once they took him to his room, they would not let me see him for several days. I said, "Every night when we talk, you need to give me a list of ten things you are grateful for that day."

His first several days it was bodily functions, much like it had been for me. Then, that amazing young man began to add things slowly to his list.

I had other tools to give him, resources he could read and listen to that opened his mind to possibilities and to the power of purpose in his life. It was that newly understood strength and the ability to see that there were options and possibilities that gave him a newfound strength to go forward.

Allow Positive to Happen

True empathy is allowing others the right to their pain, their sorrow, and their hopes and dreams. The pain and sorrow will lead you to hopes and dreams and the possibility these hopes and dreams can come true. That, my friend, is a true attitude of gratitude.

When you make the choice to put yourself in a position of gratitude, you will still have some bad days. But, when those big things happen, you will be ready to handle the unimaginable BEARS in your life that appear when you are most vulnerable and when you least expect them. Your mind will, out of shear habit, kick in, mesh the amygdala and the neo-cortex together, and make the most unbearable situations bearable.

It all starts with the attitude of gratitude and permitting yourself to experience empathy.

I wish I could say I did some of the right things that day on purpose. I'd like to say that I knew what I was doing was beneficial, or that I followed the script perfectly. I cannot.

You Can't Perform If You Don't Practice

What I can say is I was fortunate that I was already practiced.

While I did let a bad day grow out of hand, I am very lucky to have been practicing the attitude of gratitude and empathy. When the chips were down, that practiced way of life took over and put me where I needed to be. I am much more cautious with my bad days now.

I practice feeling them and giving myself permission to have empathy for myself and for others. Then I practice letting go of the self-pity.

I sincerely hope that no one reading this has ever had an experience similar to the one I just shared with you, and I hope that none of you will. Nevertheless, the truth is we all will have painful experiences in life. We can choose to have empathy for ourselves and others, or we can choose to hold onto pity and anger. Harnessing the emotional power of severely traumatic experiences is tough. It will transform your life in a way that nothing else can. Practice, so that when the time comes, you will be able to change to the positive.

These traumatic experiences are the BEARS we face. These are the dark tunnels where we either choose to crumble and give up, or move forward with hope and conviction. We can choose to search for the light and allow ourselves to have to courage to come out on the other side into a brighter world and life.

CHAPTER 8

Building Social Skills

So far in *Emotional Power*, we've established that you need:

1. Awareness
2. Attitude
3. Empathy

The fourth component to emotional power is Social Skills. We must understand, have and use appropriate social skills.

It is our social skills, or our ability to influence others, which ultimately determines how others act and react with us. It impacts our relationships, our education, our careers and everything else we have or experience.

We spoke earlier about love. To have love and to show love, you have to care for your own social and emotional needs. "Have a friend; be a friend." To do any of this, you must first have some minimal social skills. To change the way others react to you, you must change the way you react to things.

90% of us...

There are always some issues getting along with people and developing social skills. Let's look at some of the statistics.

- 90% who are negative, ornery, horrible, terrible, awful
- 90% who are no good for nothing, very bad people
- 90% who just drive us batty
- 90% have no clue they are coming across that way

While you may not have understood this until now, you now know this is true. Every one of us have said or done something that hurt or offended someone else and not known about it until months later, or longer. When we find out months later, what do we say? "Oh, no, no, no, that is not what I meant. Why didn't you say something?"

So why aren't you pointing out their behavior to them? Part of being socially skilled is having the courage and skill to tactfully tell others that their behavior is negatively impacting your relationship. Everyone makes assumptions about others' motivations. You are no different. The assumptions you make become your reality. When there is no additional conversation, that reality becomes permanent.

Remember, 90% of those obnoxious people have no clue that they are, or are at least being viewed as, obnoxious. If you just said, "Ouch!" even one time, many of them would stop.

Eye Roller

I once had a woman in one of my seminars raise her hand and say, "Dr. K, I am a recovering eye-roller!"

I said, "All-righty then, share that with us."

She said, "No seriously, I was always in trouble for having a bad attitude and I swear at first I didn't have a bad attitude. I came to work on time. I did everything that was asked of me. I kept my mouth shut."

She then said, "But over time, I did develop a bad attitude because I was sick and tired of being told that I had a bad attitude."

She told us that one day she was at home and had asked her son to do something. When she did, he rolled his eyes at her. She said that while she was seriously contemplating slapping him into tomorrow (which by the way, is the wrong response), it occurred to her he looked just like her brother when he did that. Then in a blinding flash of the obvious, it hit her, "I wonder if I roll my eyes when people ask me to do things?"

So she went to her husband and said "Honey, when you ask me to do things do I ever roll my eyes?" Her husband said, "Yeah!" and she thought, "Oh no!"

So she went to work and said "Hey boss-person, when you ask me to do things do I roll my eyes?" And the boss said, "I don't know."

But she pursued it more. She said to her boss, "Please help me out here, I have recently discovered that rolling eyes is something my family does. I was not aware of it. If I roll my eyes will you please stop me and point it out?"

E.R.A. (Eye Rollers Anonymous)

She then said it became a standing joke at work. Everybody walked around saying, "You rolled your eyes; you rolled your eyes; you rolled your eyes."

I asked, "So have you stopped rolling your eyes?"

She said "No, but we have all identified why I roll my eyes. It's my family's way of planning and processing new information."

Innocently enough, she is visualizing with her eyes her working process, where she is, where she wants to go, and the best route to take to get there.

I'll tell you what, if I was her boss or her friend and I asked her to do something, I would hope she rolled her eyes! The negative employee probably would have never emerged, had that boss stopped and said, "When you roll your eyes, I assume that you don't want to do what I have asked. Is that what you are meaning?"

That boss could have kept from labeling a good employee as negative, and later becoming so. And the boss could have kept herself from believing that this employee was negative. It was simply a misunderstood body language that led her to believe that this person was an insubordinate and negative employee.

Ninety percent of people do not know they are doing things to make us misjudge or feel badly. She was a true 90%er. Are you a 90%er? If so, what words are you uttering, or what behaviors are you displaying that may cause others to treat you in a manner that is uncomfortable, hurtful or offensive for you?

The 90% runs both ways. It could be that you are the one who is a 90%er, or it could be the other person. Either way, communication must take place so that both of you are aware. You can make conscious choices about getting along. This is how you become socially skilled.

8% = Bad Day

Eight percent of people are ugly, rude, negative, ornery, awful, no good for nothing very bad people who are having a bad day or are in a bad situation.

I just mentioned an eight percent time I had. We have all had a bad day. Some of us work in industries that deal primarily with people who are having an 8%ers' bad day.

If you work in the health industry, insurance claims, collections or customer services, you are probably dealing with the 8%ers. There are many industries where the people you deal with regularly are an 8%er. An 8%er wants your empathy. They may or may not want your help. Then they want you to leave them alone.

Their thoughts are typically, "Understand me and just let me have my bad day. I have earned it." Don't try to make their day sunshine and roses, because it may not be for them at that moment. When you have an 8%er this is when you want to duck and take cover temporarily.

Don't Fix Them

Just, duck, and take cover. Get out of their way. The 8% person, who comes across as rotten, mean and awful, typically does not mean to be taking it out on you. You are just, unfortunately, in their way that day.

With this group, you have to allow them their thoughts and emotions. But DO put a stop to any behavior that is unacceptable. The way to stop behavior is to first identify the behavior and then point the behavior out to them and let them know it is inappropriate. You can then either offer an alternate behavior or tell them their behavior will not be tolerated. Of course, all this must be done diplomatically.

When dealing with 8%ers, I'm also going to tell you to get over yourself. We have a tendency to believe we either have made or can break their bad day. Seriously, who do you think you are to define yourself as the center of their universe?

Most of the time, most of us have nothing to do with someone else's bad day. It is their bad day and their bad day alone. If you feel like you might be the cause of it, ask them, "Am I the cause of it?" If they say "yes," then you can say, "When you're ready, let's talk about it." If they say no, you can say, "Oh, I am so glad to hear that. If you need someone to talk to I'm here."

Don't stand there and tell them there is a light at the end of the tunnel, because sometimes it is just not the day for them to face their tunnel or the path for finding the light. 8%ers are simply having a bad day. They have earned it. Let them have their bad day.

2% Love It

However, if people have an 8%-day all the time, they are probably not really 8%ers. They are probably what I lovingly call 2%ers. Two percent of the people who are ugly, rude, negative, ornery, awful, no good for nothing, very, very bad people. They are that way on purpose!

There is absolutely nothing you can do about these 2%ers except be grateful that when you wake up in the morning you do not have to look at them in the mirror. Know this: It is your reaction to their antics from which they get their personal satisfaction.

Stop reacting and start acting. The only way you can do that is to have boundaries set with consequences. Boundaries must have consequences that you are willing to follow through on or they are not boundaries. Later on, we will discuss in greater detail how to do this. For now just know that with 2%ers you need to act as if you don't mind, instead of re-acting and showing that you do. If the behavior is truly bothersome, you must tell them. If they choose to not change, you must choose to accept the behavior unconditionally or remove yourself from their presence.

The numbers show that, in reality, about 98% of the people we struggle with, 98% of the people that appear to be socially unskilled, 98% of the people who believe we are socially unskilled, themselves, really don't mean to appear that way. Ninety eight percent really are good, decent, people.

You Think, Therefore, You Have A Personality

Ninety eight percent of the people are just viewing things a little bit differently than we are. Understand what makes them different is the wiring that they are born with; it's the personality style that they have. It's what makes us a 98%er to others and what makes others 98%ers to us. It is all in the wiring. We normally refer to this wiring as personality types.

Smart people have tried for ages to define and categorize personality types. You can find many different approaches. In fact, you can find an approach specific to each personality type. I've chosen a very generic categorization. One that is easy to use and easy to remember.

For the sake of our discussion, we'll say there are four core (and very different) personality styles. These four core styles are referred to in a variety of ways. They are described as colors, as profiles with letters and numbers, as animals, and many other ways. I make my personality analogy with four kinds of animals.

Some people are more right-brained and others more left-brained. Right-brained people are inclusive; they rely on emotion and emotional content to a great extent. They enjoy communication in every form, for any reason. Left-brained people are more logical. They require the information and a path that makes sense. They see communication as a method to an end.

For our right-brained friends:

They may be Peacocks. Peacocks are flamboyant, showy and appear confident. They are the life of the party and find a way to make everything into a fun experience or a game.

Or, they could be Lambs. Lambs are soft, cuddly, and provide the warm/fuzzy feelings for those around them. They truly care about your well-being and can be easily offended simply by being ignored.

For the left-brained friends:

They may be Lions who are the kings of the jungle and leaders. This type of individual needs to move quickly and swiftly.

And they may be Owls. As in Winnie-the-Pooh, the Owl is the fountain of knowledge, the know-it-all, be it necessary or not as the wise one in the group.

Where Did Your Personality Come From?

We are all born with natural wiring. That's our base preference for dealing with the world. Our wiring can change slightly according to our environment. It can also change according to our life experiences. We consciously make what adjustments we can with our wiring and change our responses based on what we learn through life. It is actually possible to suppress our natural wiring completely. But there's a danger in that. Those who choose to suppress or subvert their natural tendencies are many times viewed by others as inconsistent or untrustworthy.

There is more to communication than words, and those who are not true to their base wiring may come across as someone who is hiding something or perhaps a little fake. This is a natural reaction experienced by everyone when faced with conflicting signals.

Traits of Core Personalities

Let's examine some core traits for the various personality types.

If you are one of those that find things to be more hurtful and hold onto them a lot longer, you are probably a little bit more right-brained, more people-based, and more likely to show emotion.

If you are not affected much by what others say or do, you are probably more left-brained, more task-oriented, and considered to be more logical. You are often viewed as less friendly and unemotional until people know you well.

Remember the amygdala? We have already talked about the amygdala, the importance of having it develop, and the thoughts that go through it. Your family conditioning, that is, your early life, does seem to have an impact on the development of your amygdala. It forms your responses to events early in your life. If you were allowed to think on your own, behave according to your understanding, and were shielded from facing consequences of the behavior, you will frame events a certain way. If, on the other hand, you made choices and were allowed/forced to face the consequences of your actions, your response to events can be dramatically different.

Early life experiences help to form the structure and the responses you experience from the amygdala to the rest of your brain. We are all born with a core preference personality. As we just mentioned, with minor variances for some conditioning, we typically hold tightly to these core preferences.

Looking closely at the four animals: Everyone has a little bit of each one in them. Becoming socially skilled comes down to understanding our own dominant style and recognizing the dominant style of others. Then you appropriately communicate in the way you both can understand.

External Communications – The Core Social Skill

This is where we learn how to develop our external communication—also known as (AKA) Influence. Your social skills develop and mature from this external communication. While it is your responsibility to communicate in a manner the other person understands, equally, you must listen to them (and understand) in the manner in which they speak.

It doesn't mean that you have to become like them. It simply means you say things in a way that they will understand and that you listen in the way that they speak. Developing these skills is what will give you positive influence in your external communication. This is true social skill.

You can find dozens of scientific tests to reveal your true dominant personality style. Today, we'll experiment with a little less scientific method, though still running somewhat with the sciences. This is a "quick read" on your base personality. As with any fuzzy science, and personality definition is a fuzzy science, you should take it with a grain of salt. I suggest that if you are interested in this, you should visit some of the sites listed at the end of this chapter. Each site provides a different type of test and can help verify or refute your findings.

CHAPTER 9

Simple Personality Type Identification

BELOW YOU WILL SEE A CHART WITH FOUR QUADRANTS. THERE IS the "T" dividing the four sections. At the top of the axis, it is labeled, "needs to control more or direct." At the bottom of that axis there is, "needs to control less or indirect." On the left side you'll see, "Needs people more or relationship oriented." Opposite that, on the right side, there is, "Needs people less or more task oriented."

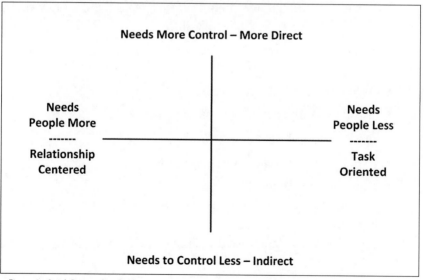

Figure 2: Quick Personality Guide

You may copy the chart or (better) recreate it on a sheet of paper. Then follow the following instructions.

Take Orders or Give Them?

Think about a person with whom you struggle. On the vertical line, somewhere between "Needs to Control More/Direct" and "Needs to Control Less / Indirect" draw an "X" where you think that person belongs.

Here is an example of how to decide where the "X" goes. An extreme of "Needs to Control More/Direct" would be:

> ‣ My way or the highway

> ‣ I am going to be in charge

> ‣ Do what I say and when I say

> ‣ Jump first, and then ask how high on the way up

That is extreme. Coming in around the middle of the upper half of the scale would be:

> ‣ "I'd like to be the leader, but if somebody else needs to be, I would be happy to let them."

OR moving just below the middle into the bottom half:

> ‣ "I would rather not be in charge of this project, but if I have to be I will do my very best to do it well."

On the bottom end of this scale, "Needs to control less and more indirect," they are going to say things like:

> ‣ I don't want to be the boss.

> ‣ Please don't make me be in charge.

> ‣ Please don't put me out there.

> ‣ You just tell me what to do. I do not want to be responsible

That is the other extreme.

Okay, so put an X on that vertical line where the person you struggle with might fall.

Now, place an M for "me." Use the same rules as above, but apply it to yourself. Put an M on the line where your preference lies.

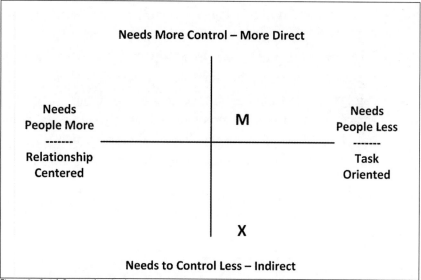

Figure 3: Quick Personality Guide.

He Who Bugs ME

For this example, the person that really bugs *me* is an extreme at the bottom of the chart. He needs less control, and more indirect communication. I, on the other hand, am up towards the top. I tend to be more direct and I like to be in charge. That is one reason I am self-employed. It makes it easier for me. When I report to someone, it is because I have chosen to do so for a short time.

Keep in mind that there is no judgment here. There is no quality, efficiency, moral or ethical component to these personal preferences. A choice here doesn't mean I am good or they are bad.

I have found that my personality lends itself, and therefore, makes it easier for me, to run my affairs personally. Likewise, it is more difficult for me to hand over control to someone else. This is something good for me to know, to acknowledge and to integrate into my personal interactions.

Need to Know or Get it Done?

Now, let's fill in the horizontal line. The same instructions apply. Here are some examples to work with:

A "Needs people more, relationship oriented" to the extreme left would be:

> ➤ "I can't function until I know everything that went on for the weekend with everybody and how they are doing today."

> ➤ "Every meeting must start with at least 15 minutes of small talk to be sure everyone is comfortable and ready to go."

Coming in to the right, but not at the middle, would be:

> ➤ "I can see that there is a problem, let's drop what we are doing right now and resolve this problem." (Still people focused)

Right of that (past the middle) more towards "Needs people less or the task oriented" is:

> ➤ "I can see that there is a problem, let me finish what I am working on and then I can give you my full undivided attention."

Finally, to the right of that is the extreme task focus:

> ➤ "Don't talk to me until all of my work is done and yours is too."

So, where does your person fall on this line? (Approximations are okay, and we're talking about an example you can think of that made you crazy.) Place your "X" accordingly.

He Who Bugs ME

My annoying person again happens to be an extreme, "Needs people more, highly relationship oriented."

I do like people, honest I do. Task oriented people love people and the relationship people do finally get their tasks done. Okay, that was a little of my bias coming out. For me, I know that if I don't finish my task, I fear I will forget what I'm doing. I am so convinced of that (much personal repetition), that my mind keeps going back to it and bugging me until I finish. I refer to that as internal nagging. I'm extremely gifted in that area.

When I am pulled away from the current task, I am not fully focused and engaged in any other conversation. While I can still be effective, it simply makes me uncomfortable. So, it is always best for me, and often for others, if I finish what I am doing, so I can give you my full, undivided attention. My "M" goes about ¼ the way from the right.

Again, this is something good to know and acknowledge about myself. It took me years to understand this. Yet, as I continue to acknowledge that this is my preference, I find that both my relationships and my work are better for it. Understanding this about myself and acknowledging this is not always the best way to interact with others, helps me modify my behavior when necessary.

Connect the Dots

Once you have your X's and your M's placed, where do they meet up?

First the X's. Start with either X and draw a line sideways or up and down until your line is even with the other X. Then draw a line from the other X until it connects with the first line you drew. Place an X where the two lines meet and draw a circle tightly around it.

Do the same for your M's now. When you finish with the M's, Draw another tight circle around the new M.

Now let's talk about what you see.

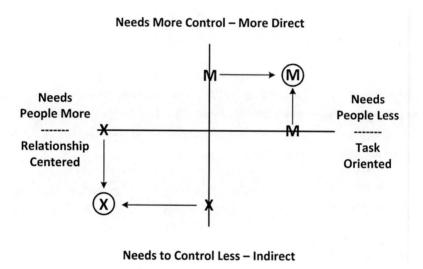

Figure 4: Sample Completed Personality Profile

He Who Bugs ME

If the person you are struggling with is in the same quadrant as you, typically they have and display traits or characteristics that you see in yourself that you don't care for. Perhaps they have traits or characteristics you have worked hard to overcome and they have not. Maybe you really just don't feel in control of your quadrant.

On the other hand, if they are in a different quadrant than you are you may just assume that the other person is a moron. Of course, they usually are not. They just see things differently.

You will notice that the person I struggled with the most is centered in the lower left hand corner. I am centered in the upper right hand corner. It appears that we are direct opposites.

Making Sense of Your Chart

This is a simple example of a personality profile.

To illustrate the quadrants and their differences, let's look at the four animals again.

The upper left, the needs to control more/direct, combined with the needs people more/relationship people are our Peacocks or our Sociable people. They are the life of the party and a 'fun to be around' person.

The upper right, the needs to control more/direct, combined with the needs people less/task people are our Lions or our Directors. This is the one many consider a typical A type personality person.

The lower left, the need to control less/indirect, combined with the needs people more/relationship people are our Lambs or our Loyal or Likeable people. The person whose shoulder you can always cry on and count on when you need help.

And finally, the lower right, the needs to control less/indirect, combined with the needs people less/task people are our Wise Old Owls, regardless of their age. These are our Analytical people who are always seeking the facts.

Assign Your Animal(s)

We each have a little bit of all of these animals within us. The wiring is there for all of them. We just have our wiring more naturally plugged in to a dominant one, and some tendencies in others. I, myself, am a Lion with Owl tendencies, forced to live in a Peacock world. Thank goodness, I originally married a Lamb or my kids would have been in more serious trouble than they were!

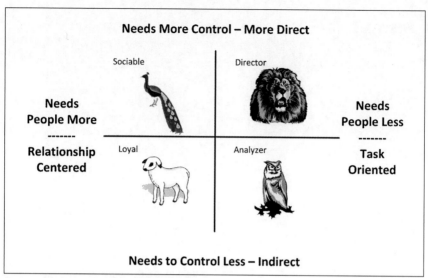

Figure 5: Personality Chart with Animal Assignments

In the next chapter, we'll go over each one of these personality types individually so that you can learn how to better communicate with them and learn how to improve your social skills.

CHAPTER 10

A Closer Look at the Animal Model

L ET'S TAKE A CLOSER LOOK NOW AT THIS ANIMAL-BASED PERSONAL-
ity model.

All four animals simply look at life differently. All four are very valuable and extremely necessary. All four have likes and dislikes, strengths
and limitations.

Once you can identify your likes and dislikes, strengths and limitations and what they are for others, you can become socially skilled and
have a positive influence on nearly everyone. Being socially skilled in
this manner will also greatly enhance your ability to convince, sell or
negotiate. You will easily do a mental shift when dealing with others,
adjust your attitude, improve your empathy and move to an awareness
that will harness your emotional power and use it to accomplish great
things.

Sociable Peacock

Let's start with Peacocks, because they wouldn't have it any other way and I don't want to lose them: They bore quickly, and I love them for it.

Our Peacocks are creative and innovative creatures.

- They are great at social skills
- They get along with others
- They are good negotiators
- They are good sales people
- They like to be out in the forefront
- Their biggest fear is not being recognized
- Their motto is: "get noticed"

"Happy is as happy does... [Peacock] people love themselves because they know exactly what they love to do and always find the time to do it."

— Dr. Taylor Hartman, *The Color Code*

When you communicate with the Peacock, it is vital that you let them know how it is going to make them look. Peacocks need to be validated, over and over and over again.

If you have a Peacock that is not being validated they will leave, mentally or physically, and go somewhere they feel more appreciated or (for them) more valued. You must appreciate your Peacocks and let them know on a regular basis why you appreciate them.

The Peacocks' Likes and Dislikes

Peacocks Love and Crave:

- Popularity
- Attention
- Constant Validation
- Challenges
- Adventure

- Spontaneity
- Excitement
- PARTY!!!

They are usually the life of the party. No party truly gets started until one or more Peacocks show up.

Peacocks will not be the ones to plan any repetitive event such as a meal-by-meal plan for the next six months. While they may have a meal plan (usually created by a Lamb or an Owl), to them, any plan is merely a suggestion based on things known in the past. Plans can and should change in an instant for any number of reasons. The main reason is, "I don't want to…"

If they feel like pizza tonight and the plan says Italian lasagna, that is simply just not close enough. If it says Chinese, it is definitely not close enough. A Peacock is most likely going to have pizza if that is what they are craving.

And between the time they decide on pizza and when it actually arrives, there may be second thoughts. I've seen some Peacocks order a pizza and be out the door to a party three minutes before the pizza arrives. You see, one downside of the Peacock's personality is a tendency to have a short attention span, and not many hard, fast, decision points.

On the other hand, if an Owl feels like Chinese tonight and lasagna is on the menu, then they are having lasagna. It is on the menu isn't it? For an Owl, the rules are made to be followed, for a Peacock the rules are, again, merely a suggestion.

Peacocks dislike, distrust, disrespect, and generally have a hard time and hate:

- **Waiting**. If you want to drive a Peacock nuts, make them wait! This absolutely drives them batty.
- **Slow, deliberate people**. The animals that most often make them wait are the Lambs and the Owls. Owls make them wait because they tend to deliberate, searching for the exactly correct answer. That slows things down. They are more methodical in their processes. They like to think about it first and then ponder the implications before they act upon it. Peacocks believe you should just do it and ask for forgiveness later. There are very few things in this world that can't be undone.

- **Tradition.** Peacocks cannot stand convention, the same old, same old. A Peacock typically sees convention as a character flaw. The Lambs, and quite often the Lions and Owls, prefer a little convention.
- **Indecision.** Peacocks will make a decision in a second. Open a menu at a new restaurant and select the dinner (sometimes for everyone) within 30 seconds. Lambs and Owls "study it to death." Peacocks go crazy over the long deliberation.
- **Lack of enthusiasm.** If Peacocks are alive, they are enthusiastic. If you ever see a "down" Peacock, take a picture or a video. It is a rare event. They believe that Lambs, Owls, and quite often, Lions are simply holding up the parade. This does not mean that those animals are actually that way. These are merely the perceptions that come across in the worldview of the Peacock.
- **Work**! If it's not fun, if it can't be made to be fun, personally rewarding, helping them to get noticed, and if there will be weeks or days, sometimes hours, of repetition and boredom, the Peacock will find a way to detach themselves from the process, sometimes to the extent of getting "sick."

The Peacock Package

Peacocks' priority in life is to enjoy it. Again their strengths are:

- Very socially skilled
- Outgoing
- Persuasive
- Risk takers
- Competitive
- Agents of change—they pursue change
- Inspiring
- Open and direct
- Love of life

They are first to a good party and if it's not good, they make it that way.

Hearing these things, Peacocks are nodding their head enthusiastically and saying, "Oh, yeah. That is MEEE!"

Their limitations can be daunting. While they can use their risk taking tendencies for positive things, that same risk mentality can have a dark side if it is not inhibited by some portion of common sense in both their personal and business lives.

Since they may not hold the other personality types in high regard, unless they put their social skills to bear appropriately, they can be viewed as:

- Reactive
- Dominating/Abrasive
- Impatient/Restless
- Overbearing/Pushy/Intimidating
- Irresponsible
- Uncommitted
- Disorganized
- Afraid to face facts
- Unfocused
- Impulsive

Hearing this most of the time our Peacock friends will be shaking their heads no and are saying, "No way! That's not me!"

Everybody who knows a Peacock, however, shakes their head and says, "Yup, yup, yup, that is how it is."

Now the Dark Side

Every personality has a dark side. When the personality abandons their core, experiences stress beyond what they believe they should be required to handle, or simply doesn't have the skills to handle the issue, they will become the Dark Lord of their personality type.

Peacocks' Dark Side includes the following tendencies:

- Jump ship
- Make light of it
- "Busy"ness, not business
- Escape in fun
- Blame others

Thankfully, most of us don't gravitate to the Dark Side. However, if a Peacock does so, you will see much of what was listed above.

The Dark Side aside, we do need our Peacocks! They are creative and innovative creatures. They are the ones that keep everything fresh and moving forward with enthusiasm. They sell our products, figure out what we need to make/create, and they are the initiators of new projects. They keep the ball rolling.

You can often tell them by their office. They are going to have several chairs and a candy dish because they want everybody to come in and hang out for a while. They will have pictures of their friends and family and almost always they will be front and center in these photos.

With our help (and some work on their part), Peacocks are critically valuable assets. They must constantly work on focus in order to progress toward the ultimate goal. Their task list, however, cannot consist of what they consider boring. They must be more aware of political implications of their behavior. Without them, there would be little innovation, few sales and little hope for a better world. And without them, who would buy the drinks after work?

We love our Peacocks. They are the ones that keep us moving forward, enjoying life and having fun with their creativity and innovation.

Sociable Peacock

Core Motivation: Fun

Fear: Not Being Recognized

Motto: Get Noticed

Natural Talents: Enthusiasm and optimism

Communication Preference:
Let them know it's making them look good
Appreciate and validate them

Likes: Popularity, Attention, Constant Validation, Challenges, Adventure, Spontaneity, and Excitement

Dislikes: Waiting, Slow-to-Get-Things-Done People, Convention, Indecision, and Lack of Enthusiasm

Strengths: Socially Skilled, Outgoing, Persuasive, Risk Taker, Competitive, Confident, Pursues Change, Inspiring, Open, and Direct

Limitations: Risk Taker, Reactive, Dominating, Abrasive, Impatient, Restless, Overbearing, Pushy, Intimidating

Dark Lord Peacocks: Politically Incorrect, Lazy, Irresponsible, Inept, Aimless

A Saying They Would Agree With:
All work and no play is missing the point!

Director Lion

The Lions' motto is "get it done" and they assume you understand that means NOW!

That's right, "Get it done, and get it done now!"

The Lions are natural managers, leads, leaders and protectors. They assume that their ideas not only make sense, but that others will grasp the vision and want to be involved.

They are amazed that anyone would question their objectives. They are also very dismissive of anything that sounds like doubt.

Lions lead the charge. They are the builders, the visionaries, and the people who can gather people to them and their cause simply by the power of their will.

> "Healthy [Lions]… are the lifeblood of humanity. They are the movers and shakers of society"
>
> – Dr. Taylor Hartman, *The Color Code*

At their core, Lions seek power. It is their motivation, their desire, and their end goal. Every project, every initiative, everything they do moves them steadily to gain more power in their lives. They first and foremost want control over their lives and then control in order to see their visions fulfilled.

They are naturals at Leadership and Vision. Where others may spend days or weeks coming up with a vision statement, a Lion will give it to you in 30 seconds. And, by the way, you'd better use it!

Lions want it done this instant because they also tend to think in branches. That is, from a single thought, several other thoughts are quickly generated. Some are valuable and are worth following up on. Sometimes, more than one should be followed up on so you get an assignment because you happen to be standing there. Those smaller branches may generate additional branches that also must be evaluated. You almost have to feel sorry for them. So many ideas and only so many heads to assign…

The moment they think of a new idea or solution, it is presented as an emergency. You sometimes hear the term, "Drive-by management," or "Line of sight management." This is a Lion at work. It's an emergency because they think so quickly, and once thought of or expressed, their thoughts immediately branch to the next logical path. The emergency is, they are unconsciously concerned they won't ever get back to that particular thought. So for Lions, it is easier to do it now, and as a manager, assign it now, than to worry if they will ever be down that path again and remember to do it later.

You can usually pick out a Lion's office because they are the ones with the nice cushy chair on their side of the desk while the one hard uncomfortable chair is on the other side. They limit their photos to one of their family. Their cubicles or offices are austere. They exude simplicity. Their communication preference is, "bullet points only." They just want the fast facts. They want you to get in, get through the one, two, or three, bullet points, get your instructions, and get out.

Lee Iacocca was a true Lion. Do you know what he would do to keep people from staying in his office too long? He would shave the front legs of his chairs just slightly so that when they sat, it was only slightly noticeable, but definitely uncomfortable. Subconsciously, people felt something was wrong with the arrangement, so much so that they would quickly say their piece and get out. He did this so they would do just that. Give him only the necessary information, and get back to work quickly, so that he could get back to his work as well.

I'm going to tell you a secret about the Lions. Their biggest fear is being taken advantage of.

When they hear that, most Lions will say, "I don't think so." But if you think about it, Lions are so afraid of being taken advantage of that they jump in and take over quickly.

When they are in charge, they are the ones doing the directing. Besides, who could possibly be more appropriate to lead?

The Lion Likes and Dislikes

Our Lions love:

- Control
- Responsibility
- Loyalty
- To look good technically
- To be right
- To be respected
- Attain approval from a select few
- Quick decisions
- Subject mastery

Lions believe that you are either for them or against them. If you are for them, you are part of their pride and they will protect you to the ends of the earth.

If you are against them, you are dinner. There is no sitting on the fence.

It is vital with a Lion that you let them know you have their back. You don't have to agree on all points or subjects, but you must let them know, if you agree or disagree that you are still loyal to them.

Lions are probably the simplest in their dislikes. They are very black and white, direct and to the point. Anything that is not black or white can be a problem for the Lion.

Here is a short list that causes them heartburn:

- Ambiguity
- Irreverence
- Laziness
- Indecisive or slow acting people
- Small talk
- Fluff not related to the task at hand
- People who take their arguments personally
- Emotional arguments

Let's look at each of these from a Lion's point of view:

- **Ambiguity:** Do you want to drive Lions nuts? This works. A Lion views ambiguity as seeing more than one side of a discussion or actively seeking more information than the Lion believes is necessary to make a decision.

To a Lion the animal with the most ambiguity is the Owl. How can this be? The Owls have all the information. While that is true, to a Lion, Owls appear to be hiding behind fluff. Lions come to the conclusion that it is because they don't really know their stuff or are not confident with their knowledge.

A Lion often believes that if Owls were confident their information was correct, they would simply state what the answer is and move on. In their defense, Owls know that the first (and usually correct) answer proposed is generally rejected by any group. (By the way, that is usually the case.)

They further believe that unless you get the picture (read, learn from them and let them talk), you may not be prepared to make the correct decision, or even recognize it when it is presented. This process is something that Lions simply don't want to engage in.

- **Irreverence:** This is a very interesting twist on the word. We'll get to the Dark Side Lord of Lions in a minute, but one of those traits is the "god complex." The Lion believes strongly that their solution is correct and most likely the only way to succeed. Therefore, irreverence, as defined by a Lion is when their decisions, goals, or authority is questioned. No one challenges god, and wins (small "g" on purpose).

Owls and Peacocks are the most prominent offenders here and to a lesser extent, the Lamb can be too. Owls really do understand the consequences of a chosen path. They probably understand the current path as well as the Lions, and have more insight into the workings of the path. Peacocks want to know how it is going to be fun. Lions think that moving down the path is fun. Lambs want everyone to be a big happy family. Lions want everyone in line and singing the same song. If you are out of step, you have two choices: 1. Get in Step, or 2. Find another army to march with.

Lions perceive that it is a display of irreverence when you ask questions about their decision, are slow to do what they tell you to do, or offer alternatives.

There is an "I" in Lion. There is no "I" in Team. Lions lead. Teams follow.

- **Laziness**: Laziness also drives a Lion nuts. Lions define laziness as not staying on the task the Lion has set or not keeping to the strict time frame provided. Lions expect progress and visible progress. To them, this is definitely a problem with the Owls, sometimes a trait of a Lamb, and a trait that a Peacock, especially the Dark Lord Peacock often displays. Remember the motto: Get it done NOW! That's not a suggestion for a Lion. It is a direct command.

  You will find that a high percentage of Owls in the IT group. On IT projects, little of the progress is visible until you get near the end. This makes Lions crazy. So crazy, in fact, that Lions have created totally new systems development methodologies to allow them to see constant progress in the project.

- **Indecisive or slow acting people**: Owls and Lambs often appear to be indecisive to a Lion. Lions expect that if you know your stuff, you can put it in place NOW. There is no allowance in their mind for customization, rephrasing, or updating. New technology should be integrated instantly if it is useful and those responsible should already know how it works.

  You can see that patience is not a virtue of a Lion.

- **Small Talk**: 'Nuf said. "Fluff" not related to the task at hand.

- **People who take their arguments personally.** This is an interesting trait of Lions. They never believe that they are attacking someone personally when they are discussing their projects. Yet, the words they use will destroy Lambs, Owls, and Peacocks. Unfortunately, it is up to the others to figure this one out. This is not usually one that a Lion will modify. The wording a Lion uses does not sound offensive to them. Should someone use the same wording or phrases with them they would take it at face value and not feel personally attacked. Because of this, they honestly believe they are not saying things offensively and are often surprised to find out that people have been offended by what they viewed as simple facts.

- **Emotional Arguments**: Don't even go there. According to the Lions, teary eyes, hand-wringing appeals to the heart, have no place in business. Should a Lion become emotional, they feel they have lost control of themselves and their situation. This is embarrassing to them. They want nothing more than to be excused long enough to pull themselves together, come back, and move on. When they see others being what they see as emotional they are embarrassed for the other person and will dismiss them. Again, because that's what they would want, they believe they are doing the "right" or "nice" thing. Unfortunately, those who were just dismissed feel as if they are not cared about or for.

Lion Strengths
- Ambitious
- Assertive
- Confident
- Decisive
- Dependable
- Goal-oriented
- Practical
- Proactive
- Responsible
- Self-determined
- Self-motivated
- Very direct

Lion Limitations
- Always right (or believe they are)
- Argumentative
- Critical
- Distant
- Dogmatic
- Impatient
- Insensitive
- Overly economical
- Selfish
- Stubborn
- Unapproachable

When they hear these limitations, many Lions are confused. They say something like, "You are saying that like it is a bad thing."

Everybody else is nodding their heads and saying "Yes, it is a bad thing!"

We love our Lions because they are the ones that take the Peacocks' ideas and bring them to fruition. Remember, our Lions like the quick bullet points, short and simple. Keep it to the Executive Summary version.

The Dark Lord

Lions are funny creatures. When a Lion is stressed, they are the only creatures that become more of their type. Here's what they do:

- Delegate
- Demand
- Cause stress in others
- Task Dominant
- More productive and successful
- Overly aggressive

My husband's father is an extremely strong Lion. At his (third) retirement party, a comment was made, "He doesn't get ulcers; he gives them!" Nothing is closer to the truth for a Lion.

As a rule, when our Lions, and quite often Peacocks, are faced with a challenge requiring a decision, their instant reaction will be "Ready—Fire—Aim!" The problem is, that for Lions, their answer will be correct 96% of the time. That simply serves to confirm their faith in their own decision process.

The Owl and quite often the Lambs, on the other hand, will react with "Ready – Aim – Aim – Aim – Aim…" These opposing approaches are often a cause of discontent and frustration between the different personality styles. Lions simply don't understand what the holdup is when they see the answer as plainly visible.

Of all of our animals, Lions are the most misunderstood. They are also the ones that understand the least. It is beyond a Lion's comprehension that everyone does not see things the same way they do. It truly does not enter into their mind that there might be another point of view. And if the thought were to rear its head, Lions wouldn't care to understand it anyway. It will just be viewed as yet another waste of time before their idea is implemented.

The Owl knows everyone will see it differently. They've analyzed it.

They probably have the "most correct" answer. The Peacocks see there are many approaches and, regardless of which one is taken, implement more enthusiastically and usually better than everyone else. That's one reason they are so fabulous. And the Lambs are in tune with everyone's emotions and needs. So like the Owls and Peacocks, they too, know we all see things differently.

Lions are not as pig-headed as people often think. They have great gut instincts and typically see what they view as the best and fastest solution quickly. The path they see is obviously logical and it simply just doesn't occur to them that their view isn't the only one.

Without Lions, few of our leaders in business, government, or any other endeavor would move the organization forward. They are the movers and shakers. They will take the chance because they have the internal belief in the "rightness" of their actions.

You gotta love the Lion.

Director Lion

Core Motivation: Power

Fear: Being taken advantage of

Motto: Get it done (NOW!)

Natural Talents:
Leadership
Vision
Communication preference
Facts only
Get to the point—Get out

Likes: Control, Responsibility, Loyalty, Quick Decisions, and Mastery

Dislikes: Irreverence, Laziness, Slow-acting People, and Indecision

Strengths: Ambitious, Assertive, Confident, Decisive, Dependable, Goal oriented, Practical, Proactive, Responsible, Self-determined, Self-motivated, Very direct

Limitations: Always Right, Argumentative, Critical, Distant, Dogmatic, Impatient, Insensitive, Overly economical, Selfish, Stubborn, Unapproachable

Dark Side: Delegate, Demand, Cause stress in others, Task Dominant, More productive and successful, Overly aggressive

A saying they would agree with:
I'll try being nicer ... If you try being smarter!

Loyal Lamb

Lambs are our relationship-oriented people. They are the glue that emotionally holds the organization together. They are the ones you intuitively trust when it comes to other people and their feelings.

Their personal rewards are based on their ability to provide quality and service, in their job, in their relationships, and their life. This means, you must not only appreciate the Lambs but must tell them often how they make a difference.

Let them know that you know what they need and want to do. Expect them to act ethically and morally. They are the most ethical and moral people you will ever know. Don't ask a Lamb to do anything questionable. They will be severely conflicted. In the end, you will lose. You will lose their respect, loyalty, and their support. The result may be disastrous for you.

They excel when they can work autonomously and feel secure in their position. You might think that working autonomously is in opposition to someone that cares deeply about others. In this case, though, Lambs are generally afraid of the conflicts that arise from close interaction on tasks, so prefer to be autonomous where possible.

Lambs have wonderful traits and characteristics. They are an incredible value to the company and society. They are the ones that remember to send the flowers.

They make up fun bulletin board notices, schedule the celebrations (and sometimes pay for them too) and have lots and lots of pictures of friends and family. They make sure birthday people have their cake and their three minutes of adoration. Lambs create that warm, friendly environment.

They adhere to tradition. And when there's not one available, they create one. If you are around a Lamb for more than three years, you will have at least six new holidays, remembrances, or other occasions that will be with you for the rest of your life (or until you and the Lamb don't see each other anymore). Still, you may receive a phone call 20 years from now to remind you about, "Our yearly remembrance pact." We love our Lambs.

"Life cannot bestow on anyone a more gratifying reward than the sincere appreciation and trust of a [Lamb as a] friend, employer, or family member."

— Dr. Taylor Hartman, *The Color Code*

Our Lambs' office is usually easy to identify. They are the ones with the nice cushy visitors chair and the box of tissue, and your favorite treat in their drawer for when you need some extra love.

While the Lion is most misunderstood, the Lamb is the one that is most taken advantage of. The Lamb's biggest fear is conflict. Their motto is, "get along."

Intimacy is a Lamb's driving factor and at the core of motivation. This isn't the kind of intimacy that leads to sex (usually), but instead it is the need to understand one's soul. They will know the things that drive you, feel the emotions that satisfy you, and learn to provide those things for you. You'll find they prefer occupations like teaching, homemaking, librarian, or jobs that allow them to be in the background, helping, making sure others succeed.

Of all the animals, Lambs are the ones that most easily reveal their insecurities. They do this with the goal of allowing others to help them become better in the areas they reveal. They are sincere in this. Be sure you include them in "The Group."

The Lamb Likes and Dislikes

Lambs love it when you love them and are loyal to them. They have likes and dislikes as well. Unlike the other animals, most of the self-image for a Lamb is based on the feedback and attention they receive; therefore, their "likes" are based on love and needs:

- Ethical behavior
- Closeness
- Affirmation
- Kindness
- Friends and family
- Being understood
- Being appreciated
- Being accepted

- Talking to you about their insecurities
- Giving quality
- Being allowed to work autonomously
- Being secure

When you work with a Lamb, it is vital you let them know how your task is going to affect other people. A Lamb has so much concern for others that they will be the one to stay late and do the work themselves instead of inconveniencing anyone else.

They would rather do it than say, "No," because they don't want conflict and they don't want to impose their needs on anyone else. In fact, there are seldom occasions where "no" leaks into their vocabulary. They would rather be taken advantage of than to disappoint another person.

But because they don't say, "No," the other animals tend to believe that the Lambs want to do whatever it is they are doing. Since the other animals have a much easier time saying, "No," if they don't want to do something or feel they cannot do it, they don't really understand how or why the concept of saying "no" is foreign to a Lamb.

So Lambs, please be aware that the assumption always will be that you WANT to do it. It will be extremely rare for the others to offer to do it for you, especially once you've said "Yes."

Lambs, you have got to learn to start saying NO! You must understand that often saying NO is actually a benefit and helps other people grow and progress. Given an opportunity, most people will let someone else do their work. Turn this around and allow others the benefit of the experience you get all the time. Quality and service are things that are only developed through practice. Those who weren't endowed with these talents must take the time to learn their benefits. Everyone becomes better and forms a more cohesive group when the work is shared and understood together.

You other three animals, you need to be careful that you don't overload a Lamb. There are downsides, and, frankly, you need the experience you are trying to pawn off on the Lambs.

Lambs' dislikes are as poignant in the other direction. Here are some of them:

- Egotism
- Contention

- Insensitivity
- Insincerity

Let's talk about these.

- **Egotism**: They dislike egotism. To them egotism is defined as someone that cares more about themselves than the communal task at hand. To them, that is usually a flighty Peacock, definitely an uncaring Lion, or even on occasion, a know-it-all Owl.

  This does not mean that the others are all egotistical; it just means that there are times the Lamb interprets their actions in that light.

  One day I had a participant at a workshop who could not decide if she was a Lamb or an Owl. She eventually decided on Lamb because she didn't want to appear egotistical. I had to laugh. I told her she was truly a Lamb and not an Owl. It would never have occurred to an Owl that they might appear egotistical just from saying they were an Owl.

- **Contention**: Lambs also have a terrible time with contention. All the animals, Lions in particular, sometimes, Owls and quite often Peacocks appear to be contentious to a Lamb. Lambs have a hard time distinguishing arguments, expression of opinions, and sarcasm. To them, they are all just rude ways of expressing oneself and lend nothing to moving forward.

  Insensitivity: Insensitivity is completely distasteful to a Lamb. It's definitely a characteristic they see in a Lion, sometimes an Owl and sometimes a Peacock. They define insensitivity as not caring about someone else or someone else's opinion. Lions know the path and don't have a lot of latitude for change. Owls have studied the path and are comfortable with it – or not. Peacocks will be offensive (sarcastic) simply because it's fun. None of these are part of a Lamb's thought processes.

- **Insincerity**: Another big no-no for a Lamb is insincerity. This is a prime characteristic of a Peacock as viewed by a Lamb. Peacocks can't walk a straight line as far as they are concerned. That big smile and the glad hand, the excitement and enthusiasm just can't be real. The other animals are viewed that way on occasion as well.

Again, this does not mean that the other animals are all insensitive or insincere, but those are how the others appear to have to a Lamb.

Lamb Strengths

Lambs have our longest list of strengths. They are:

- Caring
- Extremely helpful
- Fabulous team players
- Giving
- Good friends
- Good listeners
- Intuitive
- Kind
- Loyal
- Sincere
- Thoughtful
- Very Devoted
- Limitations

Lamb Limitations

Their limitations are maddening to the others. Look at this list:

- Overly sensitive
- Too hesitant
- Passive
- Too "other" oriented
- Indecisive
- Vulnerable
- Self-righteous
- Perfectionist
- Worry prone
- Unrealistic expectations

When they look at this list, they think, "Yes, there may be one or two things here that could have a downside, but for the most part these are good things to have."

They live in a morally correct, ethical world. Everyone is a "good person." Even those who aren't just need a little love and kindness to help them find their way. They expect that others feel the same. They make the perfect religious practitioners because they already believe strongly that there are moral rules and that Karma does truly work. Because of this, they expect others to live up to the expectation of "good people." They are a little more demanding of goodness, and appear to others to be self-righteous, simply because they are living a moral life and think others will be happier doing the same.

A couple of other actions influence their outlook. These will call into question their possible commitment to someone. So, DON'T:

- Make them feel guilty
- Expect them to forgive quickly
- Expect them to adopt change often and quickly
- Expect them to be spontaneous

The Dark Lord

How could someone so good have a Dark Side?

The better they are, the worse they can be. In the case of a Lamb, nothing can be truer. Unlike Lions who just become more intense, or Peacocks who just disappear, Lambs will make you wish you'd never met them.

The reason? If you hurt their feelings, they will most likely never forgive you. If you are disloyal, immoral, or unethical towards them or people they know, they will turn on you. They are extremely loyal until you betray them, lie to them or publicly embarrass them. At that point, you have a committed enemy for life. While you may be able to recover, mostly, by serious and honest groveling, you may never again be granted the trust of the Lamb.

When the Dark Lord takes over a Lamb, you see this behavior:

- Worry
- Depression
- Withdrawal
- Avoidance
- Blaming self and then others
- Stalking, retribution, threats escalation

The evil lies with the last two. They spend only a little time in the "grief cycle," but when they get to the "get over it" portion, they do that by hunting down the person that got them into the mess and make sure they know they made a mistake. They will not be their friend again.

Do you remember the movie, *Fatal Attraction?* Glen Close was a Lamb gone bad. Or, do you remember Cat Woman? They are scary people to cross.

Lambs are Great

But, even with a downside, what would we do without Lambs? They are the glue that holds society together. They are the ones that automatically help the poor and needy. They will take it upon themselves to build the self-esteem of others. They remember when others forget. They are our moral compass; they are the ones who care.

Loyal Lamb

Core Motivation: Intimacy

Fear: Conflict

Motto: Get Along

Natural Talents: Quality and Service

Communication Preference:
Let them know how it affects others
Appreciation for their concern
Appreciation for all they do

Likes: Closeness, Affirmation, Kindness, Caring, Friends and Family, Ethical behavior, Being understood, Being appreciated, Being accepted, Quality, Being secure

Dislikes: Egotism, Contention, Insensitivity, Insincerity

Strengths: Caring, Extremely helpful, Fabulous team players, Giving, Good friends, Good listeners, Intuitive, Kind, Loyal, Sincere, Thoughtful, Very Devoted

Limitations: Overly sensitive, Too hesitant, Passive, Too "other" oriented, Indecisive, Vulnerable, Self-righteous, Perfectionist, Worry prone, Unrealistic expectations

Dark Side: Can be the stalkers, Won't Trust, Excessive Worry, Depression, and Self-loathing

A saying they would agree with:
If you love someone, set them free. If they come back, they're yours. If not, hunt them down and kill them!

Analysts Owls

Analysts are also known as Owls. These are our personal libraries. They excel at research and fact-finding. They draw conclusions that are extremely reliable, sometimes even with little information to go on. They collect. They remember. They get it right.

Remember Spencer on *Criminal Minds* with the identic memory? Or Penelope the computer genius? And Dr. Mallard on *NCIS*, Mr. Spock, on *Star Trek*. They are all Owls. They may be science officers, researchers or artists. They are the ones who spend years developing a singularly focused talent, the lawyer, the engineer, the programmer.

They are cool, calm and collected. In a comfortable setting, they feel free to provide information at the slightest suggestion. In a public setting, however, they introvert quickly and will only share information when asked. These personality types are the engines of thought.

> *"[Owls] offer us all a model for gentle, human dignity."*
>
> - Dr. Taylor Hartman, *The Color Code*

Our Owls are easy to get along with, usually very diplomatic, and want nothing more than success for everyone around them. This group avoids conflict even more than the Lambs.

Owl Strengths

In addition to having the talent and the desire to gather information, they are among the calmest, kindest animals. You will see these qualities in a well-balanced Owl:

- Kind
- Even-tempered
- Objective
- Diplomatic
- Inventive

- Meticulous
- Practical
- Calm
- Avoiding unnecessary risks
- Exacting
- Factual
- Reserved
- Dedicated to high standards

They are extremely thorough. Can you see how others often view an Owl's strengths as limitations?

Do you need a problem solver, an out-of-the-box thinker or a fresh perspective? How about someone to move the discussion in a correct direction? That's the job for an Owl.

AND, they have a tendency to be quiet, sometimes to the point of appearing aloof. It is simply that for a large majority of them, chit-chat without purpose is simply something they don't understand. They can bury themselves in work, in research, in a hobby, or in a wild hare like no other animal can.

When they are on-task, they are single minded and totally dedicated. These are the ones that will sit down at a computer and literally not look up for four, six, eight, or sometimes ten hours. And when they do, they can't believe so much time has passed.

They have a preference for exactitude, sometimes called perfection. If you need something done quickly, unless you frame the request in such a way that there is a simple answer, and a specific timeframe involved, you will get what you asked for.

Do not; I repeat, DO NOT give a quick-turn, unknown, job to an Owl. They will analyze it to death, provide every alternative, and justify each one. After that, they will prioritize the opportunities and provide their impression of the probability of success for each. They will provide a plan for implementation of the top two or three items on the list. Finally, they will suggest not only the team (with additional resources as needed) but also the expected costs, issues involved with the implementation, and potential resolutions.

There is an old joke in the computer world that you let an engineer build a new computer only once. Because if you let them do it twice, the next time they will put in all the things they left out of the first one. Usually, these are things that shouldn't have been put in anyway. That's an Owl at work.

Right now, our Owls are saying, "That is simply not true." Everyone who knows or works with an Owl is smiling and saying, "YES, that is absolutely true."

Owl Limitations

An Owl's biggest fear is being reprimanded. Their motto is "Take time to get it right." You will often hear an Owl say, "If you don't have time to do it right the first time, when will you find time to fix it?"

The Peacock and the Lion, on the other hand, will say, "I could have fixed it seven times in the time it took you to do it the first time." They don't have much patience for an Owl's need for perfection.

Owls are not usually socially adept. They were the "geeks" in school. They didn't ever see the need for social skills because they were satisfied with their personal skills. The world they live in is rewarded through the satisfaction of getting it right and the competition of doing it better than anyone else.

When you are aware of their limitations, you understand better how to allow them to thrive. You will see these limitations in the Owls:

- Indecisive
- Silently stubborn
- Avoiding conflict
- Unexpressive
- Detached Perfectionists
- Slow to Get Things Done
- Loners
- Withdrawn
- Dull/Sullen
- Know-it-All
- Look at that list!

If you know an Owl, you will spot every one of those traits immediately:

- **Indecisive**: The owl wants more information before rendering a verdict.
- **Silently Stubborn / Avoiding conflict / Withdrawn**: Add to that, a sometimes not-so-mild disdain for those giving the marching

orders, and you get the classic passive/aggressive behavior. It's not that they mean to do it, but frankly, most of the time they already have the answer that people are looking for. They are a little disdainful that such an obviously simple answer, or such an obviously incorrect direction is even being talked about.

- **Unexpressive, Detached Perfectionists**: This is part of the same thought process. They learned long ago that if they let their feelings show too much, they will get beat up for them. Sometimes, in the past, that meant literally being beaten. These are the people that don't require, and frankly don't want, to be publicly recognized. So, when they have done well tell them, reward them, but do it in private.

- **Slow to get things done**: In many cases, they are slow because they hope their bosses, or groups, or teams, will come to their senses and realize the path they are on won't work. They move slowly when they consider the work to be "busy work" and simply not something that has any value. They are also slow because they want to be certain they have looked at the task at hand from every possible angle so they can pick the "one" option that is correct.

  At the same time, if they truly believe in the task and its timeline, their answers will be nearly perfect, and delivered as soon as they are ready, and almost always before they are needed.

- **Loner, Dull, Know-it-all**: Some of the magic of being alive is trying to figure things out. When most groups or business teams get together to figure something out, the Owl will probably have most of the information. But since they are not always socially adept, it gets lost in the presentation. Most Owls have learned to sit quietly and allow the discussion to continue until it gets to a point that the group is stuck or is looking for alternatives. At that point, the Owl will ask a question or nudge them with additional information. Owls will seldom just step in and tell people what the solution is (Even though they probably already know it).

Now are they really that way? Maybe, maybe not, but those are the perceptions that others will have. You can see where there could be conflicts with some of the more aggressive animals.

While an Owl's communication preference is, "Give and receive all of the facts, all of the details, provide all the research and where they got or are going to get their information," no one else wants to do that. Owls love to provide information, but don't want to be the presenter. The person that whispers in the candidate's ear is probably an Owl.

Pay attention to them. They understand the "big picture" and long before most people know there is even a picture. Let them suggest direction, fill in the overall picture, then turn it over to the group to enhance, discuss and decide. For truly unknown items, ask Owls do the research; they enjoy it and will be very thorough. Given time to do the research, they will seldom come to an improper conclusion.

Of all the animals, an Owl is more likely to write a 497 page report on how to change a tire. In fact, this book was less than 100 pages until my Owl editor got hold of it!

If you want your report to be read by a Lion, it should be an extremely short, executive summary, perhaps just a three-picture diagram on a single page. They don't have time to read the 497 pages nor do they care that much about the tire.

By the way, Lions are not likely to write a lengthy report either. If they have to write one, it's most likely going to be a short presentation style format with a few simple bullet points.

The Peacock will write the report and have charts, graphs, pictures, colored bullet points, music, video, and fancy section dividers on the printed version.

The Lamb is going to write it several different ways to make sure it covered everybody's needs.

Owl Likes and Dislikes

Owls live to gather information. They need:

- Information
- Consistency
- Correlation
- Perfection
- Facts
- Whole Picture information
- To be quietly valued

Owls thrive on "getting it right." Whether it's a quick and dirty answer, or a 400 page position paper, you can be fairly sure that their answer is better than good.

Remember, Captain Kirk asking Mr. Spock to calculate, in his head, the proper trajectory and speed to catapult the Enterprise around the sun and back to their future?

Spock's response was essentially, "I do not have enough information to correctly assess that request."

Kirk then said, "Spock, make a guess."

Spock raised his eyebrows, and said, "Guess?"

At this point, McCoy spoke up and said, "Spock, what Captain Kirk is saying is that your guess is better that most people's facts."

And for the Owls, that is truly the case.

Owls are appalled by:

- Arrogance
- People who take unnecessary risks
- Carelessness
- Assertiveness

Those are pretty much considered the positive traits of Lions and Peacocks.

And Owls absolutely hate fakes. Now, to an Owl, all three of the other animals can appear to be fake or phony. Surely, even those sweet, cuddly, Lambs cannot be nice all of the time!

The Owl Environment

Not too long ago, the Owl's office typically had multiple filing cabinets, and stacks and stacks of books. The filing cabinets were full and the Owl quite often had papers piled on the chairs and counters too. The older ones are still that way. The New Owls have all the information categorized and available on their tablets, with access to both personal and public databases. If they don't they can get to it very quickly and rather easily.

The Dark Lord of the Owls

Okay, here's a potentially scary person. Like the Lamb, it is possible for Owls to grow fangs. Owls show little emotion. They are an emotional sponge, if you will. They take it all in, day after day, week after week, month after month...

The more stable Owls have found an outlet for the pent-up emotions. They run, play games, bike, skydive, scuba dive, etc. They are the original, active adrenalin junkies. They need the rush to "burn off" the emotions that otherwise threaten to overwhelm them.

We have over-the-top examples of Owls finally snapping. It's called "going postal." Over the last few decades there have been shootings where the people said afterwards, "He was the nicest person, never a problem, I just can't imagine what happened to make him act like that…"

Few Owls snap like that, but many have a much lower snap-and-act mode. They take it all in over and over, and then in one, seemingly unrelated event, they snap and blow up. Whomever they are with, will be stunned. That level of reaction simply isn't justified by that small, almost insignificant thing.

The issue Owls face is that, almost immediately, they realize what they have done, the level of reaction, and the stupidity of that action. They live in hell for a few minutes to a few days until they can resolve what they did.

And, that's why when you see one of these public "postal" moments, invariably, the perpetrator will either take their own life or allow the police to kill them. They simply will not live with the guilt of a horrendous action.

So, if you want to avoid visits from the Dark Lord of the Owls, here are some things to keep in mind:

DO:
- Accept their individuality
- Create an informal, relaxed setting
- Combine firmness and kindness
- Show patience

DO NOT:
- Be cruel and insensitive
- Force immediate verbal expression
- Overwhelm them with too much
- Force confrontation

We need our Owls. They take care of our processes and procedures. They see the big picture like no one else. They provide the "correct" support, information and analysis to every business question. They make sure that we don't get ourselves into trouble.

Analyst Owl

Core Motivation: Peace

Fear: Getting Reprimanded (negative feedback)

Motto: Get It Right!

Natural Talents: Clarity and Tolerance

Communication Preference:
All the facts
Details to support analysis
Validated research

Likes: Research, Information, Consistency, and Perfection

Dislikes: Arrogance, Unnecessary Risks, Carelessness, and Overly Assertive People

Strengths: Meticulous, Practical, Avoid Unnecessary Risks, Exacting, Factual, Reserved, and Have High Standards

Limitations: Perfectionists, Slow to Get Things Done, Loners, Passive/Aggressive, Withdrawn, Dull, and Know-it-All

Dark Side: Blow up from pent up emotions, Inappropriately Angry, Seemingly Strange

A saying they would agree with:
If I pretend to agree with you, will you go away?

Story Problems

As you begin to understand things about these different animals, you now realize that they most definitely will struggle with each other from time to time. Let's look at a few story problems with the four animals:

Story: Get Paint

If you want the room painted blue, the Lion is most likely to send someone to the store for blue paint.

When the errand runner asks, "What color blue?"

The Lion will look at them as if they are an idiot and will say, "Blue," and wonder what it is about the color you don't understand.

Lions will also expect that someone else will paint the room and figures that person already knows who they are and they shouldn't have to be told.

So, let's send the Peacocks to the store, perhaps with a friend.

They will compare, and ultimately purchase, multiple shades of blue.

Then they will sponge paint those walls.

They will feel confident that it looks cool, fun, and sparkly.

The Lambs are going to contemplate which color and shade of blue is most conducive for peace, harmony and comfort.

They will stay late to paint it so the paint has time to dry before anyone arrives in the morning.

Before the Owl can even contemplate leaving the office to get paint, they must know every detail about the paint:

- The color
- The tones
- The shade
- The durability
- The guarantees
- The brand
- The size of the paint can options
- The exact dimensions of the room
- How the paint should be applied
- Who the correct vendor should be
- EVERYTHING!

Now as a Lion, I did not know that periwinkle was a shade of the color blue, nor did I care. And I certainly didn't know that there were 47 shades of periwinkle and that the various brands of paint all had different color choices within those 47 different shade options. And what is this whole deal about flat, semi-gloss, gloss—Really?

On the other hand my youngest is an Owl and if I don't tell him I want periwinkle blue in a specific brand of paint, shade number 27 in a semi-gloss he feels like I have set him up for failure.

However, if he came to me and said, "Hey Ms. Lion, I want blue periwinkle 27 in X brand paint, in a semi-gloss paint."

I am likely to say to him, "If it is that important to you, go buy it and paint it yourself." And I would probably feel like he was being condescending by giving me too many details and not letting me make a decision as to what I thought was best.

You can see where perceptions might get in the way of communicating.

We have one personality style where we are most comfortable and strong tendencies in another. For example, I am a Lion that has Owl tendencies.

Story: The Fixer

In my profession, one of the things I do for organizations is trouble shoot. This means when it is broken, I am called upon to go in and fix it, regardless the cause- hardware, software, people, or procedures. Hardware and software are typically easy to fix. You just buy new.

With people, what you must do is provide an environment that encourages them to behave differently. Part of providing that environment is finding the facts and understanding where the company currently is, where they have been, and where they want to go. You also need to know option A, B, and C for any possible changes. And if option A does not work, how do we get to option B or C?

To help a company succeed, I have to know all the details. And I am really good at gathering that information. However, once I get the necessary information, I'm back up in my Lion corner just as happy as can be. I've got the details I need as a consultant. Now I can delegate to the proper people the things that must be done. The Lion is definitely my dominant animal.

As a Lion, if I ask an Owl, "How's the report coming?"

The Owl is likely to say, "Well, we lost Ted and Susan. We are bringing in Bob and Mary."

The Lion in me says, "Okay, but the report, how is it coming?"

"Well, we are going to the library to get..."

"Will you be done Thursday at noon?"

The Owl will look at me mystified that I was just so short and curt with them and respond, "Yes, that is what I am trying to tell you!"

I think they are hiding something because they are giving me too much information. I just want to know how the report is coming. And in truth, I don't care how it's coming as much as I want verification that it will it be done by noon on Thursday.

And that's where a major difference lies. "How is it coming?" to me, means "Are you on track to deliver?" To the Owl, it means, "Bring me up to date on your progress."

For me, all I need to know is a short and sweet, "We're on track for Thursday." Know that as a Lion, I assume you will get the report done unless there was a problem. I also assume that you will tell me there is a problem if, and only if, I have to know about the problem; otherwise, you will take care of it.

On the other hand, a Lion can (and often does) drive an Owl crazy. An Owl will say to a Lion, "How was your weekend?"

The Lion will say, "Good."

The Owl, "Well, where did you go?"

The Lion, "Shopping."

Owl, "Where?"

Lion, "The mall."

Owl, "Who did you go with?"

Lion, "The kids."

The Lion is done talking. The Owl is thinking, "Give me some information!"

And the Lion is thinking, "Hey, wow, that was a really good conversation, wasn't it?" Again you can see where they may butt heads.

That same conversation with a Lamb would sound similar. The Lamb, however, will tend to believe the Lion either does not like them or is angry with them because they did not share their personal information.

And, if I had this same conversation with a Peacock, by the time you got to the word "mall" the Peacock will be telling you about their latest Mall experience and the awesome outfit they found.

Let's try this: You have all the animals at a party. The Lion has one foot in the hallway ready to escape as quickly as they can. The Peacock most likely threw the party. The Lambs are making sure everyone has a drink and hors d'oeuvres, even though it is not their party. And the Owls are standing there analyzing how much the party cost and wondering if the room is within fire regulations. You can see where they all see things differently.

Story: Travel Made Simple?

Yes, giving all of these examples are very "un-Lion" like. I'm giving various examples in hopes that one (or more) of them will make sense to the different personality types.

I worked hard on my social skills, more so now than before. Sadly, as illustrated with this next example, I discovered I didn't have the top quality social skills I thought I had.

The person with whom I struggled the most at that time was John. John is a travel agent for an agency that I often did training for. John liked to book me on multiple flights and/or on multiple airlines on any given date. Again, I am a Lion. That means, I want to get there how? NOW!

I want a direct flight, nonstop, largest plane possible because they fly the fastest. For three years I requested a permanent change in the way my flights were booked. I came across short and curt because I spoke in bullet points and these bullet point comments make a Lion sound like they don't care. Doing my best to be polite, however, for those same three years, I would very nicely say, "John please put me on direct flights. John, seriously, don't put me on multiple flights." For three years, he did it anyway.

Finally, one day as I was complaining, someone said to me, "Have you mapped out which animal he is?" Have you ever known something and not done it? I knew there were personality differences yet I had not even considered that might have anything to do with his insolence!

Embarrassed that it hadn't occurred to me to do it already, I finally sat down and analyzed which personality type he was. I was shocked. John was a Lamb! At first, that confused me. Lambs do what you want them to just to avoid conflict and they are the ones that really work the hardest to please others. I was absolutely dumfounded because I couldn't understand why he would do what he was doing.

What did I have to do now that I knew which animal he was? Remember Covey's fifth habit? I had to seek first to understand then to be understood. I understood his communication preference now, but I still had to understand why he was making my travel schedule the way he did so that I could communicate appropriately with him.

So, I said, "John, I've noticed that you tend to book multiple flights and multiple airlines on any given date. Is there a reason for this?"

He said, "Yeah."

Okay, now the fingernails down the chalkboard come out. I am seriously cringing! I tried to remain calm and polite as I said, "Okay, help me understand why."

He said, "Oh that's easy. I know the trainers gather the airline points and miles so you can use them to take your friends and family on vacation with you."

"Oh my goodness!" He had been doing it all of these years 'for me' not 'to me'!

Somewhere along the line, what had happened was one of the trainers said, "If you could just reroute us a little bit, we'd get more airline points and miles and we can take people on vacation with these points and miles." He subsequently asked a half a dozen other trainers if they'd like this, and they all said, "Yeah!"

No, he didn't ask any Lions. See the Peacocks are thinking "Party! Yeah let's do it!" And the Lambs are thinking, "Oh, that would be so nice. I can take the kids, and we can have a nice family vacation, or I can take my best friend and we can really have some bonding time." And the Owls think, "You know, it is more cost-effective, in most cases, to take multiple flights. So that's a good idea."

Lions on the other hand, don't care if it is cost-effective or if anyone goes with them on vacation. They just want to get to their current destination as quickly as possible.

Now that I understood that he was a Lamb, I could see that he needed to know what was in it for someone else. I could also understand how he would believe he was meeting others' needs. I could truly appreciate why he was thinking and acting the way he was. With these tools, I could now communicate in a way he understood and then listen in the way he spoke.

So I said, "You know John, that is really nice. I appreciate you taking the time to do that. I'd like to ask you for a favor though. It is more important for me to get from point A to B quickly than it is to have the extra airline points and miles. From now on, if it is humanly possible, could you put me on a direct flight?"

Guess what he booked me on forever-after? Yes! Direct flights. He simply needed to know what it was that I needed and/or wanted. For three years I said, "John, don't do this!" What he heard was, "Sweetheart, you don't' need to go to all that extra trouble for me!"

He, in turn, was thinking, "Karen, honey, it is alright. You are worth it. I don't mind."

All the while I am hearing, "I am completely and totally inept." We had not communicated in a manner in which both of us could or would understand.

So in this case who was the inept one, him or me? Perhaps both of us, but I was definitely not innocent.

I am 100% responsible for my part of any communication. I am not responsible for their part, but I am responsible for saying things in a way they might understand, and for listening in the way they speak.

If you learn to understand the differences and similarities in all four animals, you can understand why they deal with situations the way they do.

Story: Crying

Every personality deals differently with crying. A Lion is not likely to go into a meeting crying. If they do, they are angry at you for seeing them and angry at themselves for getting caught. They want to be dismissed. They want to pull themselves together. They want mastery and then they want to get back in to get all the facts.

The others, however, if they go in and cry, want the Lion to tell them, "Hey, it's alright."

But Lions will dismiss them believing they are being considerate, by saying, "Go ahead and pull yourself together and then come back." Again, they think they are doing a nice thing.

If you go into a Lamb's office crying they are going to hand you a tissue, sit there and cry with you. You go into a Peacock's office crying they are going to listen to you and then they are going to go, "Oh, girl, can I top that!" You go into an Owl's office crying and they are going to say, "Who, what, why, when, where and how?"

CHAPTER 11

Assertiveness

ANOTHER KEY INGREDIENT FOR EMOTIONAL POWER IS IMPROVING your external communication skills by learning how to be assertive. To truly communicate assertively, you must know the difference between passive, aggressive, and assertive. You must know and recognize the differences between the different responses and expectations of the four animals, and be flexible in the way you communicate with each. But with all four animals, you must be assertive or your message will never be heard.

Three Communication Styles

Let's look at three internal communication styles that directly affect our external communication: Passive, Aggressive, and Assertive.

Passive

Passive people tend to question:

- "Why does this always happen to me?"
- "What can I say to make them happy?"
- "What do I do to keep from causing waves?"

There is nothing wrong with asking these questions if you ask them once in a blue moon, but if that is your main mindset, you are passive.

You will be taken advantage of. Trust me on this. You don't want to be passive. Passive people are victims!

Aggressive

Aggressive people on the other hand, tend to say things like:

- "Who do they think they are?"

- "I don't have to stand here and take this."
- "What can I say to put them in their place and keep them there?"

Aggressive people generally get what they want—temporarily.

They will win the battle but lose the war because people will find a way to get even.

If you are aggressive, people will find a way to sabotage you. Even the passive people will do so.

Being aggressive is not a good place to be.

Karma will come and get you eventually.

Assertive

What you really want to be is assertive. Assertive people ask the following three questions:

- "What do I want?"
- "What do I think they want?"
- "What action or communication will get me what I want and keep both of our dignities intact?"

"What do I want?"

To some, that may sound rather selfish. But let's face it. Everything we do in life is based on that first question. Ask yourself, "Why are you nice to people?"

Some answers are:

- "I want them to like me."
- "I want to do the right thing."
- "I want to be a nice person."
- "I want them to be nice back."

I want, I want, I want… Eventually, we are all bound to get exactly what we ask for, so be careful what you ask for. Know what it is you want.

Every decision you have made in your life has led you to the place you are right now. Over the long run, your decisions have been consistent with your long-term desires.

Said another way, you are living the life you have chosen.

I often hear arguments such as, "I wanted to go home but I had to stay late!" I say, "No, you wanted to stay late."

Then we go back and forth… "No, I didn't." "Yes, you did." "No, I didn't." "Yes, you did." "NO, I did not."

I ask, "Then why did you stay late?"

The answer, "I didn't want to lose my job."

Bingo! You thought staying late would help you keep your job, and that was more important to you at that moment than going home on time.

This time, you got what you wanted.

However, sometimes you have to choose between two bad or unpleasant things. When these unfortunate situations arise, you always pick the one you want more than the other. In other words, the lesser of the two evils.

So the first question still remains: "What do I want?" It is vital that you know what you want, and that you recognize that you do have a choice. This allows you to make the right choices and decisions in the moment.

"What do I think they want?"

This is the second question assertive people tend to ask. This goes back to understanding the four animal types, Stephen Covey's "Fifth Habit," and Tony Alessandra's "Platinum Rule."

If my bosses ask me to stay late, and I don't find out why, I may believe they are just being mean, selfish, rude, or uncaring. In this case, all I see are two choices: stay late or go home. If I discuss the need a little and learn the boss needs the report done by 9:00 tomorrow morning, my options open up. I can stay late. I can go home. I can come in early. I can drop what I am doing and work on it now. I can ask for help from someone else. I can take it home and e-mail it to him when I'm done. I can ask just how important this report really is…

See how your options open up?

Your options will usually open up when you seek to understand. Likewise, as Tony says, if you don't understand what satisfies their needs, you'll never satisfy your own.

This doesn't give you the right to be condescending and give them the third degree whenever they ask you to do something. That is never the best way to go about getting information or understanding. But you do want to use your newly discovered understanding of the animal styles to ask appropriate questions and find out as much information as is needed.

"What action or communication will get me what I want and keep both of our dignities intact?"

The third question is key for positive external communication and influence.

I will share one of my favorite sayings, if I were crass enough to say it out loud. I would smile sweetly and say, "Your failure to prepare does not constitute an emergency on my part." Unfortunately, that is directly attacking the other person's dignity. This is not positive external communication. Thus, although you may really want to say it, that is one phrase that should never cross your lips.

Equally as offensive to one's dignity is saying things like, "Well, you know, I, well, I, I really have some plans, but, but, (sigh)..."

Now you are attacking your own dignity.

What you should do is say something that will get you what you want. Be sure to meet their needs as best you can and allow them some escape route, if necessary. Do this without attacking either the other person or yourself.

You may choose to say something like, "Unfortunately I have prior commitments that I cannot change I would be happy to come in early to make sure this is finished by the time you need it."

But, if coming in early is not an option, don't offer it. In fact, only offer an option you are willing to fulfill.

Some parenting courses teach this process well. People of any age tend to choose from the options given. Give two options that you want them to choose from. If you have a preference, then that one goes first, and the other is worded in such a way that it's obviously the lesser of the options.

Limiting what you offer does not take away their rights. They still have the right to go another direction, but typically they will go with the options you give them. In the business world, this is one step in the process called "managing up."

I learned this communication lesson from my younger sister when we were children. As it happened, I did not originally give the right options to my father.

I would go clothes shopping with him and I would say, "Dad, here are three outfits that I really like. Could I please have one of them?" In that case, what options did I really give him?

He heard, "May I have one or none?"

So, he would usually say, "We can't afford any of them, so put all of them back." On rare occasions, if I was lucky I might get one.

My younger sister, on the other hand, was a truly brilliant negotiator. She combined the dual choice with an assumptive close. She assumed the answer was yes. She would go shopping with our father, and say, "Hey Dad, here are three outfits I would really, really, like. I know we can't afford all three, so which one do you want me to put back?"

Go figure.

She always got one, usually two, and on occasion was allowed all three. He still had the opportunity and the right to say, "No, we can't afford any of them, put them all back," and on occasion, he did. Typically, however, he chose from the options she gave him. She directed the outcome by presenting interim choices that presupposed the end result.

Think about that. When you want something, if you can direct the steps to get somewhere, you never have to ask for the whole thing. What you ask for is a small thing that presupposes a final outcome. People are always more comfortable with small decisions.

Provide appealing options. Select your words wisely. There is a difference between can you and will you. If you say, "Can you?" in essence you are saying, "Is there any excuse at all you can come up with to get out of this?"

If you say, "Would you?" you are asking the other person if they are a nice person or not.

I learned the difference between the two from my many years of fund raising. If you ask people, can you donate? You will collect some money. You will always collect more when you say, "Would you be willing to donate?"

So, what if you say, "Unfortunately, I have other commitments that I cannot change." What do you do when they ask you what your commitments are? While it is illegal in most countries for bosses to ask you that, it could happen. (Please do not ask that question if you are a boss.)

If it is outside of business hours and they want to know what your commitments are, simply tell the truth. Tell them your commitments are of a personal nature.

If they then ask, "Are you telling me your personal commitments are more important than your job?"

You can reply with the following: "No, they are not. What I am saying is that when I make a commitment I do everything I can do to stand behind it, just as I would stand behind any commitment I made to you." It's very difficult for most to argue with something along those lines.

Here you are being assertive. By making a singular statement like that, you are not attacking the other person's dignity. In addition, you are not attacking your own dignity, nor allowing the other person to attack your dignity either.

So, let's recap the situation:

What do you want? You want to go home.

What does the boss want? He wants the report done tomorrow by 9:00 a.m.

You know the boss rarely asks you to stay late.

You want to make the boss happy.

What action or communication will get you what you want and keep both of your dignities intact?

You will get the report done before the boss arrives in the morning.

Tell him it will be in his inbox before he gets to work in the morning.

He is satisfied, which also meets what you want, because you've now determined that you want to make the boss happy.

By the way, this only works if you consistently deliver as promised. Those who keep their commitments are trusted to do the same in the future.

Side Note: If you don't want staying later or working from home in the evening to become a habit, you might preface it by saying, "You know, normally I am not available after hours but tonight I am able to do this." Or, "I can make time tonight, so I would be happy to take care of it this time."

Communication Styles Recap

Passive

- Why does this always happen to me?
- What can I say to make them happy?
- How do I keep from making waves?

Aggressive
- Who do they think they are?
- I don't have to stand here and take this!
- What can I say to put them in their place (and keep them there)?

Assertive
- What do I want?
- What do I think they want?
- What action or communication will get me what I want and keep both of our dignities intact?

Personal Scripting

With all of these verbal suggestions, you are starting to develop scripts.

As a teenager, one of my group mentors taught us the way to begin scripting. She told us, "Imagine a situation you may be in, and then imagine what your response will be. Practice that response in your head. Once you do that, your decision will already be made and you don't have to worry about making decisions based on the emotion of the moment." This is scripting, plain and simple.

Scripting is also a vital piece of being assertive. The three main statement types in scripting are: I Statements, USA Statements," and Assumptive Clauses or the If, Then, What? clause.

By the way, don't say things the way I would say it. You will probably fail miserably, just as I would if I tried to say it the way you would say it. These statements are from the heart—Your Heart.

Use the concepts you learn here, reword them and say it according to your personality and in alignment with the personality of the person with whom you are speaking.

Let's go over some scripting options.

"I" Statements

The "I" statements are the most common and are the ones that are most loved. "I" statements include statements like "I feel that...," or "I am...," "I like...," "I dislike...."

These statements portray your present state of mind in an interchange. These are fully acceptable statements because you are telling a truth about yourself. Someone else cannot attack this type of statement since it portrays your state of mind. You will find that those with less social maturity and poor self-image may choose to attack you personally for your statement, rather than attack the subject of discussion. If or when that happens, you will realize the speaker has run out of valid points, but still wants to "win" and has resorted to the last tool in their bag.

An appropriate response to a personal attack would be, "I can forgive you for that personal attack. Now, can we return to the subject at hand?"

The hearer of this statement has only one choice here. Their choice is to explain their feeling, their understanding of what is happening, or their reasoning for the item being discussed.

You may modify the "I" statements to meet your own style and comfort as long as you keep the other person in mind.

Example: "I feel uncomfortable when you talk about other people in front of me. It makes me wonder what you might be saying when I am not there. Would you mind not making comments about others to me?"

Perhaps you would like to modify the "I" statement slightly. How about this one? "I am uncomfortable when you talk about other people in front of me. Would you be willing to not make comments about others when we are together?" This "I" statement is more comfortable for some, yet still meets the other person's needs.

Both examples are equally valid. Know and use the "I" statements when they are appropriate.

For some personalities, expressing your feelings, at any level, is a case of TMI – too much information. Be aware that may be the case and take care to use emotion-based statements sparingly.

I don't do well personally with the "I" statements. When I hear somebody say, "I feel, when you... because..." to me, it sounds like a personal problem. If they, however, remove the feelings and insert facts, and say, "I am...," such as, "I am confused," then it is easier for me to identify with the situation.

Again, this goes back to me being a Lion who prefers the facts versus the feelings. To me, "I feel confused," sounds like an emotional concern that you should resolve on your own or get over. The statement, "I am confused," could still be a personal problem that's tied closely to an emotion, but by saying "I am" I can see that you have already identified the emotion brought up by the issues and have accepted responsibility for them.

Many of you may not see it this way. That goes back to the idea of understanding how others see it versus the way you see it. The same is true, however, about the way I say it. If I must, I do show respect to what the other three personality types like. They may need to hear the "feel" part of the "I" statements. There will also be times when even I need to hear or say the "I feel" statements to make a valid point.

That being said, just because my comfort is in the factual rather than the emotional, I do not have permission to force the other person into factual comments when they are expressing how they feel. My responsibilities again are to Speak in a manner the other may understand and to Listen in the manner in which they speak.

"USA" Statements

Next are the "USA" statements. I love the "USA" acronym and philosophy. "USA" statements are the statements I use most often. Here is the breakdown:

U – Understanding statement
S – Situation reference
A – Alternative action, statement, option

U – Understanding statement

These are statements such as, "I understand," "I can appreciate," "I am aware that," or simply, "unfortunately." That last one, "unfortunately," is your way of saying, "I understand, but it is not going to happen."

An understanding statement could also be a statement of fact without judgments. "Barbara when you're late for work..." With that phrase, I'm saying, "I understand you are going to be late." I am not judging that activity, nor am I complaining about it, I am just making a statement of fact.

S – Situation Reference

What is the situation at hand? "Barbara when you are late for work, it puts me behind in mine and I have to work longer to get caught up." Okay, that is the situation. It is putting me behind, and I have to work longer to catch up.

How could you use this with the earlier scenario with the boss asking you to stay late?

"Unfortunately, (the U) I have other commitments that I cannot get out of (S)."

Before we go to the A in USA, I'd like to point out that you may use either two or all three, of the steps in USA method. You should always use the first, "I" statement to set the conversation context and disallow argument about the initial premise. Then you may follow this with either, or both, of the S and A comments.

A – Alternative

This is the Alternate Action or Option you are offering or asking for.

The statements together may sound like this:

"Barbara, when you're late for work, it puts me behind in mine and then I have to get caught up. If you need to come in late for work, I will ask Susan (that's the boss) for additional help in the mornings. What do you think?"

Saying this may not make Barbara very happy, but you have respectfully given her fair warning and kept the communication lines open by asking her for another option. There are no secret punches being taken; there is no hidden agenda. In short, you are being assertive or straightforward. Being straightforward is much better than saying nothing to Barbara and then telling Susan that Barbara is always late. In that case, both Susan and Barbara will deem you as a tattletale, and they would be right.

What if you don't want to tell Susan that Barbara is late at all? It is quite possible that is not the route you want to take.

Remember the first question: What do I want?

If tattling is not an option for you then you need to ask yourself, "What action or option am I willing to offer?" Perhaps it's,

"(U) Barbara, when you are late for work, (S) it puts me behind in mine, and then I have got to get caught up. How about a deal? (A) I will cover you in the mornings until you can get here, then you cover for me in the afternoon for the same amount of time. Would you be willing to do that?"

This option is allowing Barbara the choice of being late, as long as she does what is necessary to keep you from paying the consequence for her actions. Some companies would not allow that arrangement. In fact, that arrangement could result in both of you being fired. So, be smart in making these types of deals. Never do something that could end in you being viewed as the wrongdoer. Always put ethics and honesty first.

With the boss scenario, perhaps you might say,

"(U) Unfortunately, (S) I have other commitments that I cannot get out of. (A) But, I would be happy work on it at home or come in early to get it done."

Or perhaps you might only use the U and S.

"Unfortunately I have other commitments that I cannot get out of."

We've outlined a couple of different examples. The verbiage you use will depend upon the situation and the personality styles you are working with.

If, Then..., What?

I saved my very favorite assertive communication tool until last. It is the good ol' assumptive clause. I love, love, love, the Assumptive Clause.

You do have to be careful with the term "assumption" however. Many are uncomfortable with that word. The "assumption" word is not the singular word, nor the word you must use. I am just calling this tool the "Assumptive Clause" because you are making an assumption regardless of the term you use to describe it. Many refer to this as an "If, Then…, What?" clause.

For me the Assumptive Clause is simply: "When I see this behavior, I assume or get the impression that (fill in the blank). Is that the assumption you want me to make?" Or, "Was that your intent?," or, "Am I interpreting that correctly?"

You may use the Assumptive Clause" without using the word assumption. For example: "When you roll your eyes it tells me you don't agree with what I have asked you to do, is that what you mean?"

Or perhaps you will use "assumption," as in, "When you slam the door, I normally assume that you are angry at me. Is that the assumption I should be making?" Another example, "When we are talking, and you turn around and walk away, it makes me think that you don't care about what I'm saying. Is that correct?" Both of those examples are simply asking for clarification.

With the Assumptive Clause, I am pointing out only the behavior. I am then stating my interpretation of the behavior and then finally, I am asking for clarification, such as, "Have I interpreted correctly?"

Whether they say yes or no to your interpretation, you are now set to ask for help in understanding their intent. You are also set to diplomatically point out undesirable behavior on their part.

The Assumptive Clause works well for me. Remember, this is a Lion speaking. It may not work as well for some. For me, a simple yes is sufficient. I don't need the underlying justification. Others may. That is why I give you three options. Find the one that works best for you and the person with whom you are communicating.

Soft Assertion

Before moving on, I must add one last thing on being assertive. It is easier for others to not feel attacked when you use your "Please pass the butter" voice. Please pass the butter. Now that sounds ridiculous but think about it for a moment. If you are at a nice restaurant and you want people to continue to be impressed with you, you are not going to yell, "Hey! Moron! Butter! HERE!" Though I must say, I do hear these same kinds of things at work and at home, and actually from time to time at the restaurant. They come out as, "You want me to WHAT?" "What part of NO don't you understand?" "Hey! Moron! Butter here!"

Passive is Not Appreciated

My favorite non-effective statement is the passive, "Wow, I bet my roll would taste better if I, if I, had some butter on it." What is that all about? Do you want the butter or not? Saying it that way does not leave a clear understanding of the action you are hoping for!

But I hear these kinds of things at home and at work as well. You may hear someone at work say "Well, if I just didn't have to answer the phones I wouldn't be so far behind." And the person whose phones you are answering says, "I know, aren't they awful?"

That is when most people want to smack the other person on the head and say, "Hello! That was a strongly worded hint!" Do yourself and the other person a huge favor, don't hint! People don't get it, and even if they do, they pretend they don't.

Oh, my ex-husband was the king of this at home. When I first started traveling with work, our kids were in their mid to late teens. My ex, in frustration, would stand in the kitchen and say to the kids, "I wouldn't be so stressed if I just had some help in the kitchen."

The kids' typical response as they walked away was, "Yes, I know."

When I'd get home he'd say, "Those children of yours (they are ours)..."

I would then ask the kids why they weren't helping their father, and they'd tell me he never asked.

"What do you think he was saying?"

"Oh, we thought he was hinting he wanted you to hire a maid." Again, IF they do get it, it is real easy to pretend they didn't.

So, you are at a nice restaurant, you'd like the butter, and you want people to continue to be impressed with you, simply say, "Please pass the butter." Try it. "Please pass the butter." Hear the calm cadence to it. There is a calm cadence to please pass the butter that says I am in control of me. Therefore, I am in control of my part of the conversation. I am not in control of you or your part of the conversation, nor do I want to be.

Using the please pass the butter voice, try, "Barbara when you are late for work..." Can you hear the calm cadence? Or, "Unfortunately I have other commitments..." (The calm way in which you say it plays a big part of being assertive.

Assertive Recap

Again, the three questions you ask for being assertive are:

1. What do I want?
2. What do I think they want?
3. What action or communication will get me what I want and keep both of our dignities intact?

Social Skills Review

We have gone over several ways to improve your social skills. Let's review:

- You will improve your social skills by understanding what animal personality type you most closely match and what animal the person you are dealing with most likely matches.
- You increase your social skills by improving your assertiveness and communication skills.

- Scripting allows you to preplan responses. By understanding what the different characteristics for the different personality types, you can create specific scripts for how you might best deal with each.
- It is vital that to continue to develop social skills to make best use of your emotional power. In all things, your social skills can make or break relationships, negotiations, and even your emotional power.
- However, by developing superior social skills, you improve on all of these things. With properly developed social skills, you know how to provide an environment that encourages others to behave in a manner that is conducive to success for both of you. This is also known as influence.
- With improved social skills, you will have emotional power that you can now harness for your use in your relationships, for your career, and for all your future successes.

In the next chapter, we will talk about another critical element to harnessing your emotional power—managing your emotions.

CHAPTER 12

Managing Your Emotions

L IMAN ABBOT SAID, "DO NOT TEACH YOUR CHILDREN NEVER TO BE angry! Teach them how to be angry."

Component number five for harnessing your emotional power is managing your emotions. People have emotions. The key is not suppression. Suppression leads to pressure which leads to explosion.

I do not teach people to suppress their emotions. Rather, I teach them how to deal with their emotions and how to use those emotions to their benefit. Let's learn how to put your emotions to work for you.

Managing in Five Steps

There are five steps for managing your emotions. There is no correct order. You can crisscross, start at the top, start at the bottom, or go in any direction you want, but there are five steps, and you must complete them all. They are:

1: Identify

Recognize you are experiencing an emotion. Identify the emotion you are having and understand the root cause of that emotion:

- What thoughts are you having?
- What emotion are you facing?
- What is creating it?
- What behavior, comment, event, circumstance or thought has happened to create that emotion?

You must identify all of these things.

2: Communicate

I'd like to repeat some information from the Introduction on communication because it sets who you are, what you think, the emotions you experience and how you behave.

In life, there are two types of communication: Internal and External.

Internal communication is called programming. There are 1500 words per minute whizzing through your brain, telling you who you are, who you are not, what you can be, what you can do, and what you can have.

We determine our own internal communication by constantly reprogramming what we allow ourselves to believe and think. To become more positive, we must supplement any negative influences in our lives with positive influences and positive thoughts. Positive thoughts will change our internal programming. Positive programming leads to emotional strength. Positive thoughts yield positive results. Our personal logic engine learns best through positive reinforcement. It, in turn, provides a desire for additional positive experiences.

External communication is called influence. It is the ability to communicate with other people in such a way they want to give you what you want. We develop positive external communication by developing our own personal social skills. Later in the book, we will learn appropriate ways to develop social skills that will benefit us as well as others.

Many have been taught since youth what others deemed as socially acceptable behavior towards others. These lessons, however, came at the expense of personal positive programming. Negative programming has become a common societal practice. We are constantly bombarded with politically correct phrases like the following:

- Be humble.
- They think they are so great (said in an accusatory way).
- Who do they think they are?
- Don't be so competitive.
- You are no better than the next guy.
- You need to lose weight, be more attractive, sacrifice your time and money, etc.

Any one of these comments can be valid at any given time. But when they are used as a general catch phrase, they become a sticky substance that will glue us to negative programming.

We can change our programming by choosing to have a mental shift. Shift your views. Shift your thoughts. Get the most out of life.

Our programming—both positive and negative—directly affects our thought processes. Our thought processes determine our emotions and our emotional responses.

Be consciously aware of your internal and external communications. Your internal communication sets how you view things. Be fully aware that your perception of shared events will probably not be the same as others. Your external communications determine how others view you.

It you think about it, this is so true. Pretend I am a fully carded, stamped and true feminist. George walks in to the office. George is known to be a little of a ladies' man. He walks right up to me and says, "My, my, Dr. K., you are looking ravishing today."

Well, as a feminist, I would necessarily take offense. My internal communications would be awash with negative stereotypical responses. "Who does he think he is?" "What gives him the right?" "That comment was degrading," and more.

My outside persona might darken a little, and if I were kind, I'd probably say something like, "George, you are a misogynistic flirt who needs to be slapped down. Please keep your opinions to yourself."

If I was not a flaming feminist, my response might be, "Why George, what a nice thing to say. Thank you."

Which do you believe is the more correct response given what you have learned?

Perception is the key. The things that you believe will become true and will literally change reality to make the events fit your reality.

I would submit that while you may have the right to be offended, taking offense is, in itself, offensive. Release your fear, anger and resentment and drop the self-righteous requirement to become offended.

Talk to yourself (out loud if necessary, pretend you're on a Bluetooth) and convey the thoughts that will create the emotions you desire. Keep the thoughts and talk positive. In another publication (a CD), I talk through several hundred positive personal affirmations. (You can find that link in the appendix section of this book.)

Fill your mind with positive influence. When you run into a challenge, attack it in a positive light. You'll be surprised how much better the resolution is.

We often hear, "Communicate with other people." But, unless you are willing to admit what you are feeling and communicate it internally, it is pretty hard to communicate an unacknowledged feeling with someone else. You must communicate both with yourself and with others.

3: Change

You may be required to change the way you look at things. Other people do have valid thoughts. Required is a strong word. Let me re-phrase:

Should you desire to improve your social skills, a change in the way you view the world around you will be an incredible benefit.

You may also have to change the way you feel about things, the way you see things and do things. In fact, you have to become comfortable with change, embrace it, and use it. Even (shudder), become a change agent!

Many people are uncomfortable with change. Most avoid change because it requires going through all the stages of grief. We go through the stages of grief no matter how big or small the change is.

I once saw a seminar presenter ask the people in their audience to sign their name in their notebook with their dominant hand. Most complied. Once the group had signed their names, she asked them to yell out answers to these questions: How did that make you feel? What were you thinking while you were writing?

People called out things like, "I felt nervous, annoyed, powerful, comfortable and indifferent." Or, "I thought my writing was pretty, ugly, scribbly, etc…"

She listened to each in turn and nodded her head in agreement. Then she paused, looked at the group and said, "Now, put your pen in your non-dominant hand."

In the room, you heard people, gasp, giggle, groan, moan and complain. Some put their pens on the table, and folded their arms across their chest, refusing to do it.

She just stood there silently, looking at the people in the room with a knowing grin. After several moments of protest from the group, she said, "Did you all hear that?"

The group looked at her puzzled. "What?" they said.

She continued, "Did you hear all that mumbling and grumbling, all because I asked you to hold your pen in a different hand?"

She then continued. "I did not say you needed to sign your name with your non-dominant hand. I only asked you to put the pen in your other hand. From the fear or anticipation of change, you all reacted. Some of you giggled from discomfort. Others rolled their eyes from seeing no sense in the activity. Most complained in one fashion or another. A few of you absolutely refused to do anything that might resemble something outside the norm. You just gave up and put your pens down. And, a very few of you simply put the pen in your other hand."

That was a great object lesson.

If the majority of people react that poorly to that small of a change, imagine how they are going to react when there is a large change facing them, especially one over which they have no control.

The best way to get comfortable with change is to start changing things up on a daily basis. Go to work using a different route. Take the exit before or after the one you normally take and then backtrack. If you wear mascara, tomorrow put the mascara on the opposite eye first. If you put on both socks and then both shoes put on one sock and then a shoe and then the other sock and a shoe. Walk into a room backwards. Okay, that may be a little too silly for many, but you get the idea; just do something different every single day.

It does not matter what kind of change it is, you will go through the five stages of grief:

- Shock
- Denial
- Anger
- Bargaining
- And finally, Acceptance

Your personal perception of the magnitude of the change determines how quickly you go through these stages. You will go through those stages much faster, however, if you practice purposefully going through them on the small things first. Then, when you are faced with a BEAR, and one of the big changes is before you, you are in a much better position to deal with it.

4: Anticipate

Remember Scripting? This is one reason for it. You must anticipate responses before you ever experience the event. This means anticipate your response physically and emotionally as well as other people's responses both physically and emotionally. Know and anticipate their responses to various situations and script accordingly. When you script, try planning for these multiple responses, not just for the one you think people are most like to give. Remember, you could be wrong about them.

Also, anticipate success. This ties back to changing your internal communications. Instead of always expecting the worst, start expecting and anticipating the best.

A good friend of mine has a saying that I love and have adopted when anticipating an outcome. It is, "Always ask for what you want. The worst thing that could happen is you get what you ask for. Then you have to make a decision—do I really want it. If you don't get what you've asked for, you are no worse off than before. If you don't ask you definitely won't get it. Ask and you most likely will."

She anticipates success from asking for what she wants and typically gets it.

Thoughts are very powerful! Never underestimate the power of thoughts.

5: Be Flexible

You must be flexible. This means you communicate so the other person can understand and that you listen in the same manner that the other person communicates. It doesn't mean you have to become them. It does means you have to flex your communication style to understand them and to be understood by them.

CHAPTER 13

Six Vital Keys

We've hit briefly on the five steps for managing your emotions. Let's also look at six vital keys that go along with these five steps.

Key 1: Understand Your Emotions

You must understand the role you have given emotions in your life. How important is each emotion? Does it paralyze you? Does it move you forward? You have a tool to move forward when you know and understand emotions. Without emotions, you cannot make correct decisions for yourself.

I heard of a gentleman who had to have his amygdala removed. The doctors thought this would be a great opportunity to study how quickly he'd make decisions because his emotions would not get wrapped up in the decision making process.

The results from this study were surprising. The man could not make a decision. He did not have a gut instinct to tell him which one was the right choice for him. In fact, all of our decisions are emotion-based. We make an emotional decision based on our personal value system. Then we spend time creating a logical scenario that justifies that decision. When you become more emotionally stable, you can then take another look at the logical results of your decision. This gives you the ability to throw out that initial decision and logic in order to build a better decision when necessary and appropriate.

Every decision you make has an emotion involved at the outset. Why did you wear what you have on today? Emotions: I look good and I feel good when I wear this. It feels comfortable, etc. Logic: It will protect me from the elements. If we went just off of logic, we could just as easily wear nothing but a blanket when we go to the store. Logic and emotion together deems that without appropriate clothing we may feel embarrassed by not meeting the social norms. Perhaps you are fearful of arrest for indecent exposure. Some may have a thrill of the shock factor. You get the idea. No matter how logical a decision is or is not, there is an emotion somehow attached to that decision.

Key 2: Thought Control

The second key for managing your emotions is control of your thoughts. We not only can, but always do, control our thoughts. The current from our thoughts to the amygdala identifies the emotional assignment given.

Have you ever heard the defense, "I just got so mad that I flew into a rage and couldn't help myself?" Or maybe this one, "I completely lost control and don't remember a thing that happened?"

You now know that your behavior is a learned process. If you are one who rages, who has a hair trigger, makes men, women and children cringe, or mistreats small animals… Somewhere along your life's path, you came to believe that rage helped your cause. So, you practiced. The more you practiced, the better you got. Now, you are nearing perfection at rage. So, instead of people flocking around you, and adoring you, there are some noticeable gaps in your circle of friends. How is that working out for you?

We are still alive today because we can identify our character faults and reprogram our thoughts. If you have behaviors that result in short term benefits and long-term failures, seek them out and substitute them. Then, work as hard on them as you did to get where you currently are.

Stop for just a moment and think of something that frustrates you. Ask yourself, "When I experience that, is the person doing it on purpose? Should I or could I choose to look at this situation differently?"

Perhaps if you chose to create a mental shift, as we discussed earlier, it will make managing your emotions much easier for you, and much more bearable for those around you.

And, where do these behaviors start?

Right, with your thoughts.
- A thought enters your mind
- Your auto-response (that's a habit) clicks in
- You go down a path that has worked for you before

When it turns out that path is not a good one, you really must take some time to evaluate the thought that put you in this autopilot response.

What is that thought trigger? Can you remove that current auto response by replacing it with something else? Will a deep breath help? Maybe humming a tune? Maybe just a three-second pause before you act. What will allow you to evaluate what just happened before you go on autopilot again?

For every action, there was first a thought that you decided to act on.
- Some thoughts do not warrant taking up valuable space in your brain
- Some will always lead to pain
- Some thoughts should be redirected
- Some thoughts lead to actions that are no longer appropriate for you in the life you now live

Identify your thoughts. Align them with the type of person you are now and put the right thoughts in place for the person you desire to become.

Key 3: Identify your emotional triggers

This is very similar to the thoughts in Key 2. What sets you off? What do you allow to annoy you? What do you allow to frustrate you? What exactly is it that is angering you?

Maybe a source of your annoyance is a bad driver, or maybe it is a co-worker that snaps her fingers all the time, or maybe it is somebody who is always tapping their fingernails on a desktop. Is it the person that is triggering the annoyance or is it the behavior? Of course, it is the behavior.

We've established that emotion is initially triggered by initial thoughts routing from the subconscious to the amygdala, which then lead to conscious thoughts and our actions (our own behaviors). Now it's time for you to start identifying what thoughts and emotions you have allowed to control your life.

Emotions control your life! They do. They do for everyone to some extent. Some wear them on their sleeve and others hold them very close. In any case, the key, and the reason you are reading this book, is to learn how to use those emotions effectively.

> *An emotional trigger is simply a learned response to an event, internal or external, that causes an emotional response for you.*

Know yourself. Identify and understand your personal triggers that lead to unwelcome thoughts.

> *An unwelcome thought is something that leads you to anti-social behavior, at any level.*

If necessary, you can first identify the most acceptable responses, and work backwards to link those triggers to correct thoughts and proper actions.

Key 4: Monitor Physical Responses

The fourth key to managing your emotions is monitoring your physical responses.

- Do you blush?
- Do you sweat?
- Does the vein on the side of your head pop?
- Do you get all choked up or cry easily?
- Do you withdraw?
- Does your voice get squeaky?
- Do you get various types of headaches?

Learn your physical response to each emotion.

As you begin to identify these, you will be able to intercept emotional responses that you recognize as precursors to unwelcome actions when they first start coming on.

Here is an interesting question. What physical response do you have when you are frightened?

- Does your heart palpitate?

- Do you get knots in your stomach?
- Do your palms get sweaty?
- Do you have a shortness of breath?

Now, what are the physical signs of excitement? Something you are looking forward to?

- Your heart palpitates
- You get butterflies (also known as knots) in your stomach
- Your palms get sweaty
- You may even have a shortness of breath.

The symptoms of fear and excitement both look and sound pretty much the same, don't they?

Here is a mind trick that works: When these systems come on, instead of letting fear paralyze you, identify the physical responses, and tell yourself instead that you are excited for the opportunity to try something new. Your mind is already half way there; it just needs a little push.

Key 5: Prepare for tough emotional situations

It is true that often you don't know when situations are going to be tough. You don't know when they are going to hit. You can't even begin to imagine what may or may not happen in many cases.

Don't become paranoid that your world is going to fall apart around you. Instead, prepare for the little hiccups, plan time to review the events of the day by looking at how you felt and how you dealt with them. Also, on a daily basis, plan, and prepare to hold onto hope should you ever face a mountain sized obstacle.

Keep writing in your gratitude journal. When that tough situation suddenly, and often unexpectedly hits, you are in a better place naturally because you have practiced it over and over again. You will be more emotionally powerful.

Key 6: Manage in the moment

In other words, recognize the trigger, actively direct the thoughts, evaluate the proposed action, and revise as needed.

If you are angry, ask yourself:

- "What exactly am I angry at now?"
- "What are the primary emotions?"

- ▪ "What is the core emotion?"
- ▪ "Why do I think that my automatic response is valid this time?"

Then manage those emotions. You more easily manage emotions from big events in the moment if you have taken the time to practice on the little things on a daily basis.

Ask yourself, "How do I really feel, and how do I want to respond to this?" You cannot suppress your emotions for long. And you should not. But you can and should direct the thoughts and the actions that your emotions generate.

You do not have the right to "lose control." The biggest cop-out in the world is, "He/She made me angry." No one can make you anything unless you release control to someone else and agree to be that thing. No one else controls your behavior.

You manage responses to emotions instead of letting emotions control you. You do that by controlling your triggers and your thoughts.

Your initial thoughts, based on internal or external input, create an emotion. Your response (action or behavior) to that emotion flows from habits you have created that have been acceptable to you in the past.

Six Keys Summary

So here are your six keys to Managing Your Emotions:

1. Understand the role you have given emotions in your life
2. Control your thoughts
3. Identify your emotional triggers
4. Monitor your physical responses
5. Prepare for tough emotional situations
6. Manage in the moment

CHAPTER 14

Monitor Your Physical Responses

I'M GOING TO TAKE A LITTLE MORE TIME ON KEY #4, MONITOR YOUR Physical Responses. These are the primary factors that other people use to judge you. Active control of your physical reactions leads the perception of others that you are the type of person that will remain cool, calm, and effective through any scenario.

As we said before, you manage your physical reactions first by understanding physical responses to each emotion. Then you identify the best path to reroute the triggers and thoughts allowing you to eliminate that initial physical reaction.

You may be thinking, "My competence is being questioned." The emotion behind that is panic, fear of discovery, or self-doubt. Perhaps that leads you to the physical reaction of crying, yelling defensively, or blushing.

In this case, once you can find a way to bolster your confidence of your competency, the fear goes away, self-doubt decreases, and you don't panic. This results in no tears, yelling, or blushing.

Or, perhaps, you can come to realize that what you are identifying as a personal attack on your abilities is nothing more than a request for help, a desire to understand, or the other person's personal preference for communication.

The Owls usually lack social interactive skills, so when they ask a question, it very often sounds like a personal attack. The Lions will cut you off in mid-sentence. The Peacocks will be off on another subject before you can finish your answer. None of those indicates their opinion of your competency, yet, depending on which animal you are, your initial response could be, personal self-doubt, anger, tears, or simply resignation. You have to realize that sometimes, it is not all about you.

Tears

Let's take a closer look at tears for a moment. We may respond with tears to a variety of emotions. What is it that brings you to tears? It may be anger, happiness, sadness, joy, guilt, or embarrassment.

How do you control tears? Both men and women can and do shed tears. Historically however, tears outside of sadness are more commonly linked to children and women.

The men and women who tend to cry often say, "I can't help it, they just come. It is so embarrassing." They may ask, "How can I stop?"

Well, there are several things you can do to keep those tears from coming, but the first thing is stop telling yourself, "Do not cry." Change your thoughts to a positive choice such as, "Do this or do that." By the way, this is also a great trick when dealing with children. Tell them what to do instead of what not to do.

We Don't, You Don't

Your sub-conscious cannot process negative commands. When you say to yourself, "Do not cry," what the subconscious hears is, "Cry. Cry. Cry." Our subconscious simply does not compute the phrase, "Do not." Negative format commands have the opposite effect. I'm about to prove this to you.

Here we go: Do NOT picture the color red, in fact, pick any other color, but DO NOT see the color red. Don't picture a red dress, or a red fire truck. Don't visualize a red ball, or a red apple. No red stop signs or lights. And, whatever you do, do not see anything that resembles the color red in any way in your mind.

Hey, I said, "Do not see red."

Let's be honest. Did you visualize something other than red things?

Some people already know how to control their thoughts. Maybe you are one of them. Maybe you were actually able to change the objects to see blue, green or yellow. Even if you were able to force yourself to visualize other colors, that red was probably the first thing you saw. It kept creeping in. Another important point to make here is that you saw every one of the things that were mentioned, even if you were able to change the color.

That was called redirection or sublimation. Since we were talking about colors, the things were classed as "safe." It was okay, you felt you could visualize the dress or fire truck. It was the color you concentrated on. This is a powerful point of negotiation and influence: Sometimes the point you are focusing on is simply a cover under which the main point is hidden.

While you can force yourself to see other colors, you have to be extremely focused to ignore that particular external stimulus, especially when you were told beforehand to look for it. Telling yourself, "See green," works. Telling yourself, "Do not see red" simply does not work.

You now know, "Do Not," will give you the opposite reaction from the one you want. So, instead of telling yourself, "Do not cry," what is it that you can say when you feel the moisture coming?

Tear Analysis

Before we give the alternatives, let's first understand the physiology of tears. Dr. William H. Frey II, a biochemist at the St. Paul-Ramsey Medical Center in Minnesota made an interesting discovery about the content of tears.

He and his team analyzed two types of tears: the emotional ones (crying when emotionally upset and stressed), and the ones arising from irritants (such as crying from onions).

They found that emotional tears contained more of the protein-based hormones: prolactin, adrenocorticotropic hormone, and leucine en-kephalin (natural painkiller), all of which are produced by our body when under stress. It seems as if the body is getting rid of these chemicals through tears.

Some articles on tears suggest that the cause for adults crying is more often emotional duress rather than physical pain. Some state, whether it is intentional or not, you cry to solicit assistance, be it in the form of physical aid or an emotional solace.

You also know that for the benefit and physical health of our eyes, tears are continually produced in small quantities by the tear glands. Tears are evenly spread over the surface of our eyes as we blink to clean and lubricate them. Some of the tears evaporate, but the remainder is drained into the nose through the tear ducts.

Minimize The Tears

Your tear ducts are on an angle. When under emotional or physical stress, as tears begin to form in your eyes you tend to tilt your head down. The act of tipping your chin down and looking down closes the tear ducts (your drains) and all that extra moisture begins to puddle on your lower lid. It only holds so much. At some point, usually sooner than later, it overflows, rolls down your cheek, and drips off your chin and the tip of your nose.

At this point, most of us are embarrassed to be caught crying. That makes it worse. Women unfortunately, more so than men, will go from embarrassment to mortification. The embarrassed crying jumps directly to a mortified sobbing mode. That just makes it worse. You don't want to go into the sobbing mode because now you are beyond embarrassed and beyond mortified that you are caught sobbing, And that will cause you to cry even harder.

This is when we typically start telling ourselves, "Do not cry. Do not cry." Subconsciously, we are already a wreck, so that "let it loose" program is fully activated and all we can focus on is cry, cry, cry… and we do.

Tilting

So, what do you do if you feel the moisture starting to form? Here are a few stop-the-tears tricks. Instead of tipping your chin down, pull your chin up just slightly, open your eyes wide and look up. I don't mean tip your head way back and look up at the ceiling, I mean just look up slightly and open your eyes wider. It opens the tear ducts slightly, and lets your eyes handle the initial overflow and drain appropriately or evaporate, instead of spilling over.

Another trick shared by some is to do some kind of an analytical, left brain activity. You can do math, you can add, you can subtract, you can count backwards, you can recite the alphabet (backwards). Anything that is analytical will stop those tears from coming.

Toothpick

I was recently told a trick that I have now tried out a couple of times myself. Pretend you are chewing on a toothpick between your front teeth. You won't tear up!

I have found this works for both the emotional and irritant tears. I have tried it cutting up potent onions. I placed a toothpick between my teeth, cut the onions and didn't shed a single tear. The next time I tried it, without thinking, I rubbed my eyes, with an onion soaked hand. Amazingly still, no tears. I could smell the onion but the tears did not run.

Tight Ass

Here's another trick that sounds silly and, quite frankly, is a indeed a little silly. I have not tried it personally. But I've had many people from all across the world swear by it. They tell me if you feel the moisture starting to form, tighten your buttocks. Yes, that is what I said. As I said, it sounds silly. I don't know the science behind it, maybe tightening one area will tighten the tear glands too.

I've been told that tightening any round muscle in your body actually tightens them all. So, in theory, pursing your lips or pretending you are sucking on a straw could have the same effect. But, if you use the largest round muscle in your body, the effect should be more apparent.

Water, Please!

There is another trick that I do use quite often, and I do know this one works. If you think you are going to be in a situation where the tears are inevitable, and you don't want to cry, take a glass of water with you into the meeting or conversation and slowly sip on it. That's right, just sip on the water. Again, I have tried this many times, and it works.

Unstoppable!

So what do you do if you try the different tricks and the tears come anyway? You know what? Sometimes it does not matter what you try, those stubborn tears will still fall. At that point, the best thing you can do, and the most powerful thing you can do, is acknowledge them to yourself and to others. Remember, tears are a cry for help. Let the other people know what you expect or need from them, and then move on.

If you can acknowledge that you are crying, both to yourself and to other people, it puts you and the other person in a less helpless and more helpful position.

As a general rule, people aren't quite sure what to do if you start to cry. They are usually thinking, "How do I react to this person?" It calms the situation if you tell them what you expect or what they can do. Go ahead and say, "You can see that I am crying." They can now say to themselves, "Whew, now I don't have to point out that they are crying. They've already figured it out." This sounds silly, but have you ever been asked if you are crying even as the tears roll down your face?

Once you've acknowledged the tears, tell them what the best thing to do about tears may be. Perhaps this is where you suggest that they can or should focus on something else. Or say something like, "We are going to move on," or "Please ignore the tears and let's focus on the facts."

They now have something else to concentrate on, and no longer have to fear what to do or if they are doing the right thing. This circles back to telling people what to do instead of what not to do.

As was illustrated in our opening story about Pearl, you can show emotional power through tears. It is not the tears themselves that make people find you powerful, but the conviction behind your tears. I firmly believe it wasn't the tears that the group saw streaming down Pearl's face that gave her the power that day, but I believe it was because they saw the strength in her convictions. They saw the strength of her emotions. They saw strength and power behind her words because SHE saw it as strength instead of as a weakness.

She told them, "You can see I feel strongly." You can use the same tactic with any emotion. "You can see I feel strongly about this. Please ignore my frustration. Let's focus on the facts." "You can see that this is embarrassing for me. Please ignore my blushing, and let's keep talking about the proposal." "You can see that I am upset. Please ignore my red face, and let's work toward a solution."

Use the directive speech pattern in the way it was meant to be used. But acknowledge that, yes, I am doing something. Yes, this is what you can do about it, and yes, let's keep moving on.

Pearl acknowledged the tears to herself so she didn't have to go into the sobbing mode and then try to cover it up. She acknowledged it to other people. She told them effectively, "You don't need to worry about the tears, I have it under control." Now they could stop worrying about the tears. They could stop worrying about her state of mind or perhaps her frailties. Instead, they could focus on the things they needed to focus on.

Yelling!

Yelling is another emotional reaction that both men and women face. This often stems from the same thoughts, emotions and justification as tears. Though anyone can yell this is an outburst that more often is linked to teenagers and grown men.

Many of the tricks for tears can work when you feel the need to yell rise. You can do some kind of an analytical, left-brain activity. You can try humming, or take a deep breath, count to ten or even pinch your fingers together.

I have discovered over the years that the people who yell often may intimidate those around them temporarily, but they lose respect and authority in the end. The yelling is linked to a belief or judgment by others that the person yelling is either unable to control themselves or that they are a bully.

People who yell often lose their effectiveness. From time to time, it may be necessary or appropriate to yell. You may yell to inform someone of danger such as yell at a child to get out of the way of an oncoming car. If a raised tone is something that people are used to, the impact is lost and the information is likely ignored when the tone is raised for an appropriate reason.

One of the most powerful tools I have found to make an impact is the opposite of yelling. If I will soften my voice and calmly speak to someone, they are more likely to respond.

It is remarkably rare for anyone to hear an angry raised tone from me. Since my "please pass the butter" voice is the norm, on those rare occasions when yelling to make a startling point is necessary, the intent and impact is definite and immediate.

I do want to reiterate that should raising your voice outside of cheering, ever be used, it must be on an extremely rare occasion. So rare in fact, most cannot remember the last time it happened or remember it ever happening at all.

Keep Calm

What are some of the other physical reactions you might have? Some people clam up. Many see clamming up as a weakness or even as manipulation or punishment towards the other person. The Clam may see the behavior as a self-preservation response, possibly eliminating a more overt reaction that would be less acceptable. Many Clams prefer the Clam to yelling, crying or throwing things.

What can you do if feel you are going to clam up? If you know you clam up under certain situations prepare yourself ahead of time. Have scripts ready in advance and practice them, practice them, practice them. If you practice the scripts, when you are calm, then when that time comes that you are not, and you feel yourself starting to clam up, think about one of your scripts. With a practiced script in mind you will slowly start to relax and say what needs to be said in a more appropriate and acceptable fashion.

One of my colleagues prepared and practiced her comments for when someone disagrees with her. She says, "That is a view I hadn't yet considered. Give me some time to think about it then let's finish this discussion." She says this one statement has saved her many arguments and has kept her from clamming up or shutting down all together.

Overreact?

Let's look at acting as compared to overreacting as a method to help subdue our physical reactions.

When do you overreact? Many people overreact because they are afraid. Sometimes, I too, need to think a little bit more before I react so I won't overreact. Like my colleagues, I too, have practiced a few standard scripts that I have become comfortable using.

Now, when situations arise where I previously may have reacted negatively, I can calmly call upon the appropriate script. This allows me to act instead of overreact. I may say something like, "Well, you know that is one way of looking at it," or "Let me think about that for a few minutes." Or I will say, "Well, that is interesting. I like that point of view. Would you be willing to listen to another point of view as well?"

I am validating them for their point of view, I am not agreeing with it necessarily, but I am validating it and I am giving myself time to share my information so that we can both make a conscious decision on what we want to do.

As for the physical reactions to emotions: Yes, you will have physical reactions. Some, you can reroute through different triggers and thoughts. Some you never will. You can accept that as a fact, but not before you have actually spent a good deal of time resetting the action.

Changes through Emotions—Adrenalin

Let's look at changes that are brought on by emotions. When you become stressed and highly emotional, your cortisol levels elevate in your brain. That attacks the hippocampus. Serotonin levels elevate. Your anxiety level increases and adrenalin will begin to pump.

Adrenalin in small doses is healthy. It keeps your body ready for action. A small bump every now and then is a type of "fire drill" that keeps the body in tune and ready for "the big one." But when you are continuously overdosing on adrenalin, it wears you out. It will attack you and can cripple you physically and psychologically.

You must take time to understand what happens to you physically when you are going through various emotions. Once you do, you can ask yourself, "Is this healthy for me?" The answer is always a simple, yes or no.

If it is, great! Crying is healthy, and it is therapeutic. Laughing is healthy too, and it is also therapeutic. But, understand, you must evaluate your reactions to know if it is healthy or not. Are you doing it in a manner, and at a time, that is congruent with what you want it to convey? The real question is, "Am I aware enough of this emotion to be managing it effectively?"

Anger and Physiology

Other emotions can create major problems for us. Anger is one that tends to get us into the most trouble. We have already talked about anger. Did you know that it takes two to eight hours to recover at a cellular level from five minutes of unresolved anger? This is a massive hit to your system.

We've gone over the idea that anger can be good, and we have discussed the negative aspects of it as well. How do YOU react to your anger?

I like what Buddha said, "Holding onto anger is like grasping a hot coal with the intent of throwing it at someone else. You are the one who gets burned."

So, what do you do with your anger? How do you respond to things when in an angry state? How do you display your anger?

- Does that vein on the side of your head pop?
- Do you turn red in the face or cry?
- Do you get short and curt with your coworkers and/or friends?
- What kind of comments do you make?
- Does your voice rise?
- Does it shake?
- What is it that you allow your anger to do to you?

Only you can know. When you become aware of what you do with your anger, you can then ask yourself, "Is that really going to help?"

The next thought should be, "How can I view this situation differently so that I can respond and react differently?"

Happy, Happy, Joy, Joy

No one "makes" you do, feel or be anything. People choose to be happy and have joy, or to not be happy. You are people. You make a choice.

Hope Jackson says, "Happiness is a form of courage."

For ultimate strength and impact, you may want to question your physical response to joy as well.

- Do you cry?
- Do you beam from cheek to cheek?
- Do you smile?
- Or are you one of those people who forget to tell your face you were having a good day?

Do other people respond to your joy the way you intended or had hope they would?

There are people who just cannot bring themselves to show any expression of joy whatsoever. While others will say that they are irritable and ornery, they might actually be quite happy that day.

They have just forgotten to tell their face.

Show your joy! If you are one who forgets to tell your face you are joyful, practice in the mirror showing joy on your face so that others can share in the joy with you.

Joy is contagious. It will rub off on other people.

I am talking directly to those who just read this and said, "I don't think so." Change is the most difficult thing in the world. Change for the better. Start now.

Practice and have the courage to show your joy. Others will find joy in being near you. It is not arrogant, vain or cocky to have and to share your joy. Some are afraid that it will make others feel less fortunate. This is just silly. We need to see gleaming eyes, beaming smiles and happiness to refuel ourselves.

CHAPTER 15

Willow, Weep For Me

W E HAVE LOOKED AT ANGER, WE HAVE LOOKED AT JOY, BUT WHAT about sorrow? Hubert Humphry says, "Oh my friend it is not what they take away from you that counts, it is what you do with what you have left."

What do you do with your sorrow? It doesn't matter what people take away; it is what you do with what is left. They always leave something. They don't have control over your mind.

Dr. Victor Frankl wrote *Last of the Human Freedoms*. He is my hero. He swore he was going to save millions of lives and he has.

As a young man, Dr. Frankl was in the Nazi Prison Camps, where, they used the prisoners to perform "studies" on the human reproductive system, on the effects of sleep deprivation, dehydration and other hideous, horrible crimes. People all around him were dying.

He observed that their death, in many cases, did not come from the torture, but came because they had simply given up. One day while being tortured, he realized:

> *"We who lived in concentration camps can remember the men who walked through the huts comforting others, giving away their last piece of bread. They may have been few in number, but they offer sufficient proof that everything can be taken from a man but one thing: the last of the human freedoms— to choose one's attitude in any given set of circumstances, to choose one's own way."*
>
> — Viktor E. Frankl

He decided that day that he was going to live if it was possible in any way, shape, or form, and he was going to help others.

After enduring the suffering in these camps, Frankl validated his hallmark conclusion, "Even in the most absurd, painful, and dehumanized situation, life has potential meaning and that, therefore, even suffering is meaningful."

This conclusion served as a strong basis for his Logotherapy and existential analysis, which Frankl described before WWII. He is quoted as saying, "What is to give light must endure burning."

They're your choices, not your circumstances:

> "Forces beyond your control can take away everything you possess except one thing, your freedom to choose how you will respond to the situation. You cannot control what happens to you in life, but you can always control what you will feel and do about what happens to you."
>
> – Victor Frankl

In life, there is joy and there is sorrow. So what can you do with your sorrow?

- Sometimes cleansing comes from crying
- Sometimes you have to laugh
- Sometimes you laugh until you cry
- When sorrow leads to an angry state of mind you might scream or yell

As long as you use your sorrow to move you towards resolution, using it to help yourself find the exit to the tunnel, it is okay.

It is okay to have a heavy heart and keep the gratitudes as best you can. Choose how you react. Choose to find happiness even in sorrowful times.

Managing, Rather than Being Enslaved

Managing your emotions IS how you Harness Your Emotional Power.

Managing your emotions comes down to understanding the emotion you are experiencing.

Is it a good stress or a bad stress? When one is stressed over a long period of time, the amygdala becomes enlarged or swells. As it does, it reacts similarly to the way a sprained ankle might. If the ankle swells and somebody comes up and starts to flick at it, it will hurt. When your amygdala swells, your thoughts start pinging off the walls. At this time you most likely will overreact. When stressed, your thoughts amplify and your emotions amplify. Unfortunately, if you are not real careful, both your actions and behaviors amplify.

The best way to manage your stress is to know yourself and the new self you are continually building. That knowledge hinges on your core values and your knowledge of your emotions.

We are going to do a little exercise. This will help you discover your core values.

For the exercise, you'll need a sheet of paper. A normal sized, blank, writing paper will be fine. Writing in this book will not work. This is a hands-on activity so please get a piece of blank paper.

Uncover your core values

With your blank paper,

1. Please fold it in half two times: once side-to-side and once top to bottom.
2. When you have done that, unfold it.
3. You should now have a piece of paper with four quadrants: two across and two down.
4. In each of these four quadrants, write one thing that is important to you at this point in your life.
5. If it is your children and you have three children, that is one quadrant total for the children, not three quadrants, one for each child. Put "my Children" in one section.
6. Write something else important in the other quadrants.

These are your items. They can be anything. I've seen lists containing: children, friends, family, religion, money, health, career, chocolate chip cookies, horseback riding, golfing, a hot car, whatever.

It is up to you. Seldom are any two lists the same.

These should be the things that matter the most to you, right now. Please, don't put what you think should be important. You are not doing this to please someone else. Be sure to put what actually is important for you, right now. Again, just one thing in each section—a total of only four things, clump it the best you can.

Some of you are saying "Only four?' but what I see most often when sharing this activity is people saying, "Holy cow! I don't have four things!"

I want you to give yourself a couple of moments to come up with all four. It is vital that you have all four written down before we go on.

You may need a minute.

OK. I'm going to trust that you have done that. If you haven't, don't let excuses stop you. Take a minute and get it done now. This doesn't work if you don't have four really valid things you care about.

Four

Now that you have all four items written down, you have just identified your core values. If you don't like these, if they are lightweight, if they aren't "really" what drive you, if you would have chosen something else had you known what we were doing, THEN you are making excuses and you are in denial. Because, at this point in time, these were the things you came up with. These are your core values.

Core values are the most important things to you at this point in your life. The items you listed are the things you must focus on first, everything else can wait. So, focusing on these things first, with the less pressing things coming second, is going to relieve a vast amount of your stress and set you more quickly on that path you ultimately want to follow.

Have you ever noticed that life happens? Life is what happens when you are making plans. When life happens, many times, we end up giving away one of the things that are most important to us.

Let's see what this looks like. Take your paper and tear off one section. Make it the one section that you are willing to give up right now. Just tear it right off. Come on, as painful as it may be, tear off a section you can give up.

Okay, I can hear the whining and groaning! It is just an activity. Come on, quit whining, make the choice and tear it off. Tear it off. Yes, I have had grown men and women come to tears over this activity. But it is vital that you do this to fully appreciate what we are learning.

Three

Okay, now you only have three sections left. As illustrated with the paper, you are no longer whole. By removing this one item, you have created a hole in your life. It kind of feels like getting kicked in the gut, doesn't it? Have you ever had the wind knocked out of you? When that happens, you tend to gasp for air and when you gasp, you get less air. Right now, many of you are gasping for life because you had to give something up.

You gave it up, because you didn't plan your life, you let life plan you. Please plan your life. Don't let life plan you. If you don't plan your life you are going to end up giving away one more of those sections. Go ahead, tear off one more section. You can do it.

Ouch! That was painful. I know some of you are holding on and saying, "I am not willing to do that." Just tear it off. It is just an activity. You can get a fresh piece of paper when we are done, I promise.

Two

With two sections gone, you are now left with half a life. If you don't plan life, life will plan you. This is where resentment, anxiety, guilt, remorse, feeling overwhelmed, depression, all of those things start to come in because you have given away half of your life.

You feel resentful towards the people that are causing you to spend your time in other places, and towards the events that are causing you to lose your valuable time. You may feel resentful towards yourself. You will often even begin to feel resentful toward the people that you wanted to spend time with, but gave up.

You have got to plan your life because if you don't plan life, life will plan you. You know what I am going to make you do next don't you. You get to keep one. You decide which one you are going to keep. I know that it is a hard decision but just keep one and you DO get to keep it. I am not going to make you give away that last one.

One

Now that you have selected one, take the other three and throw them away. Just get rid of them. No, you may not keep them. Crumple them up and throw them in the trash. Yes, you can get a fresh piece of paper when we are done, but for now, get rid of the other three sections.

The one you kept is obviously the most important thing to you, right now, in your life. Yes, that's right. The mere fact that it is still in front of you, dictates that it is THE most important.

Now that you have honestly identified the most important thing in your life right now, here is what I want you to do. Don't worry, you get to keep it. Write down on that piece of paper how much quality time you currently spend on that thing every single day.

If your section says your children, I do not want you to write down the time it took you to cook dinner for them. That is not quality time. Quality time is talking with them at dinner about how their day went, teaching them how to cook dinner with you while you talk about important things, shooting hoops, or maybe working on homework with them. Those are examples of quality time.

Maybe None

I had a lady one day who said, "I sleep next to my husband. Does that count as quality time?" NO. You are asleep. Quality time would be when you spend your time talking to each other, being actively engaged, not just sleeping.

A few of you are saying, "Score!" or "Yes! I kept the right one." What I have found, however, is most people are saying, "Oh my goodness, I gave that one up too."

When I told you to take one section off people balked. They say, "No way! I am not willing to give one up."

When I tell people to take the second one off, they will look at me like I am a seven-headed harpy.

And when I said that you only get to keep one, people fight. It is usually only out of resignation they finally say, "Fine. I'll tear it off, 'cause I am going to go write them all down again anyway!"

Actually None!

When it comes down to it, and you're honest with yourself, have you really given up all four of these things that are most important to you?

Many of us have. In my opinion, this is the leading cause of unhealthy and unnecessary stress in your life. Most stress is the result of unrealized expectations, or incongruent life choices.

Simply put, your sub-conscious knows what's good for you, and what brings you satisfaction and joy. It does a lot of nagging when you don't care for it correctly. This is called Stress.

You. Are. Under. Stress. Which. Is. Completely. Unnecessary!

This example was crafted to show you how much stress you are actually experiencing in your life. You most likely found that after you threw away the three quadrants you released, you actually felt a little better.

When you came to realize that even the one you held tightly was not being treated as if it were the priority item you say it is, that there was something basically wrong with your personal prioritization process.

If you throw away (or ignore) that last quadrant, then it was not really your life priority. Perhaps you need to do the quadrant thing again, this time being a little more honest with yourself.

As I said, the point of the exercise is to illustrate stress levels in your life. It is the things that you know should come first, that you don't put first, that cause the majority of your stress.

While some of these are the result of childhood experiences, learned behaviors or simply poor choices, the fact remains that you are where you are now because of the choices you have made, good or bad.

By now, you realize that it is time to plan your life. Letting life plan you is just not working.

So, how do you know if you are under too much stress?

There Are Signs…

There are physical signs and there are emotional signs. If you have more than three of these signs, you are at a point of danger where you really must make adjustments.

You grind your teeth. And yes, if you have a child that grinds their teeth in their sleep, you need to reevaluate their life style. I had a client one day tell me, even their dog grinds his teeth. Okay, they really need to reevaluate the entire household.

You get headaches. "But I am prone to headaches," you say. Are you sure? It's very possible that you have been stressed for so long that you have just accepted headaches as part of your life.

Tired. "But I didn't sleep well last night." Yes, and what were you thinking about? I have yet to meet anyone that could honestly say, "I could not sleep last night because I had nothing to think about." You are usually worried about something, stressing about something, and your mind is going a million miles an hour.

Stomach. You have gastrointestinal problems. Yes, that is what I said, gastrointestinal problems. You may get ulcers, or have cramps. Some will become backed up or get the runs. Both can kill.

Stress You Out

Stress overall, just makes us plain sick. Hundreds of studies have measured how stress impacts our immune systems and fights disease.

> *"Ohio State University... found that students under pressure had slower-healing wounds and took longer to produce immune system cells that kill invading organisms. Renowned researcher Dr. Dean Ornish, M.D., who has spent 20 years examining the effects of stress on the body, found that stress reduction techniques could actually help reverse heart disease. And ... a leader in the field of psychosomatic medicine, found that metastatic breast cancer patients lived longer when they participated in support groups."*

Stress has been found to be a leading cause of heart diseases for women. "Mental stress and depression affect women's hearts more than men's. Depression makes it difficult to maintain a healthy lifestyle and follow recommended treatment, so talk to your doctor if you're having symptoms of depression."

The only known cause for uterine cancer is estrogen dominance. Guess what one of the leading causes of estrogen dominance is? Stress. The common cold, the flu, etc., etc. You cannot afford to have too much stress because it will make you ill.

What are some of the emotional signs of dangerous levels of stress?

- You are short tempered
- You are grumpy
- You cry easily, okay, you cry easier than normal
- You lack concentration. This is two-fold:
1. You can't focus on anything at all
2. You obsess over one thing and cannot let it go

Then there is depression in all of its forms:

- Fatigue and decreased energy
- Feelings of guilt, worthlessness, and/or helplessness

- Feelings of hopelessness and/or pessimism
- Insomnia, early-morning wakefulness, or excessive sleeping
- Irritability, restlessness
- Loss of interest in activities or hobbies once pleasurable
- Difficulty concentrating, remembering details, and making decisions
- Overeating or appetite loss
- Persistent aches or pains, headaches, cramps, or digestive problems that do not ease, even with treatment
- Persistent sad, anxious, or "empty" feelings
- Thoughts of suicide, or suicide attempts

"But Karen I have a chemical imbalance." I will grant you some people do. If you are under an excessive amount of stress however, the stress will make any chemical imbalance much worse.

When under too much stress, the chemical reaction to medications will vary. If you can eliminate the bulk of your stress, any chemical imbalance is much easier to take proper care of with the right medical attention. You must watch and control the stress.

Now that I have truly stressed you out, let's look at some easy ways to deal with stress.

CHAPTER 16

Instant Calming Sequences (ICS)

I PROMISED TO TELL YOU SOME EASY WAYS TO DEAL WITH STRESS. There are some temporary, quick and easy fixes to stress. Note with the words, "quick and easy," also comes the term, "temporary."

There are longer-term fixes and we'll deal with those later.

First, the Quick Ones

These are called instant calming sequences, also known as ICS. Instant calming sequences are simple. I've practiced doing instant calming sequences for a number of years now. I can calm myself down instantly in most cases. This first one is the one I catch myself doing the most.

The body-sway

You can always tell in the grocery store line the people who have had children or babysat because they tend to sway back and forth or move from one foot to the other. That is the body-sway. In case you don't know, we do this because it calms us, not the child. It calms us, and when we are calm, the child is calm.

A quick example: I actually like sitting next to the screaming child on the airplane now. You probably just went "Okay, she is clearly strange." But you know what, unless that child has an ear infection I prefer to be the one sitting next to them because I know I can calm them down. On the other hand, taking a child on an airplane that has an ear infection is simply abusive to that poor child.

The typical crying child does not cry because of anything other than their parents are stressing and freaking out. And the child can feel it. The more the child feels it, the more they cry.

So, I will do a couple of instant calming sequences. I will calm myself down and then I will say, "Here, may I try?" as I hold my arms out. The parents may freak out at this point because some stranger wants to hold their screaming child. It's funny though, they always give them to me. I take this crying child and calmly hold them for two to three minutes and the kid will stop crying. If I hold the child for five to ten minutes, they will almost always fall asleep. Feeling safe in a calm environment (in this case in my arms) helps the child to relax. Rarely does a relaxed or calm child feel the need to cry.

How do I do it? ICS – The body sway for starters along with a few of the others ICS techniques.

Palm Stroke

Some people will rub their hands together. Some their palms together, others will rub the fingertips across the palm of their hand. I put my hands together and rub the pad of my thumb across the palm of my hand, not because I am stressed, but just because it is overall relaxing.

The hands are some of the most sensitive organs on your body. There are actually nerve connections to other major body parts and organs here in your palms. Thus, this palm stroke will affect your entire body.

Deep Breathing

For this, you breathe deep on purpose. When you do this, you breathe fully. Be sure you fill your lungs thoroughly each time you breathe. Breathe deep breaths, filling your lungs and expanding your abdomen. Deep breath, exhale slowly. Deep breath, exhale slowly. Well, you get the idea.

I took voice lessons as a youth and they would make us practice bringing our hands up by our mouth and pulling our hands down toward our abdominal area and up as though it was filling the lungs and then back towards the abdominal area and back toward our mouth. To this day if I find myself overly stressed, I will catch myself just doing a short hand movement for bringing the breath down and it reminds me to breathe deeply.

Do you breathe deeply naturally? If you are in a position to, try this: Put one hand on your chest and one on your stomach. Now, let's take three deep breaths together. Ready? Breathe in deeply; exhale fully. Breathe in again even deeper. Exhale slowly. And now one more time real deep, breath in, hold it, breath in some more, hold it, exhale. Okay, if the hand on your stomach was moving, great, you did it right. If the hand on your chest is the one that was moving, you are breathing inappropriately. That is what we call shallow or chest breathing.

You are born breathing down into your abdominal area, but as we age, and I don't mean 30-40-50, I mean at that ages of 9 to 12 or 13 we begin to move our breathing higher, into our chest. We begin to shallow or chest-breathe. You are literally suffocating yourself when you do this.

When you shallow or chest-breathe and then you talk, you sound nervous even if you are not. And, since you aren't getting a "full" breath, you are also suffocating your brain. Do you believe you can be thinking as productively and as critically as you could be? Easy answer: No.

So, with continuous shallow breathing, your brain is not thinking and functioning properly and your body is not healing and recovering. You are slowly, sometimes rapidly, destroying your entire system.

It is vital that you learn to breathe.

Here are a couple things to try. Lie on your back on the floor. Put a small stack of books on your stomach, and as you breathe in, push the books up. As you breathe out, be sure the books float down. You should not be forcing your stomach down, just let it happen naturally when you breathe out. This will get the right muscles working and give you a feeling for what "proper" breathing feels like.

Another exercise to try is bending over and pretending you are sucking peanut butter through a straw. You cannot do that in your chest, it hurts too badly. Learn to bring the airway down into the abdominal area.

Tighten and Relax

This is a favorite of hypnotists and self-hypnosis. This is a great ICS to use with stress balls. You squeeze and relax, squeeze and relax. Hands, feet, legs, stomach. Any portion of your body works.

Here's a learning tip: When you get stressed, the muscles in your neck, shoulders, cheeks and jaw tighten. When they tighten, it tells your brain, "I'm stressed." Your brain then says, "Oh, my goodness, you are stressed," and it tightens muscles even more. This is a biological response from our ancestors. They experienced stress when they were hunting or being hunted. Your brain is preparing you for a fight or to run. Have you ever heard of "Fight or Flight"? This is it. Your stressed body is now ready for instant action. Unfortunately (or fortunately) our "civilized" lifestyle doesn't typically have these do or die situations. I hope none of you ever do. Without the fight or flight however, there is no stress reliever for our system. We spin up, and stay that way.

If you practice tightening and relaxing, what you are doing is keying your body that the stress point has past. You match the tenseness and it tells your body, "Okay, I know you are tense, but now it is time to relax." Your body will slowly, not instantly, begin to accept the relaxing action and eventually will relax itself.

Now, I don't actually go around squeezing stress balls, but I can stand in front of a group of people and pinch my finger and thumb together, rotating the action from hand to hand. Standing or sitting I can tighten my belly, and most people won't even notice. You can curl and uncurl your toes. There are a variety of things you can do to tighten and relax, tighten and relax. As you do this, the muscles begin to relax, and your stress level decreases.

Laugh

Another instant calming sequence, and probably the most important one for me–well all three of these next ones are the most important ones for me, but let's start with this one: Laughter

You must laugh for five minutes a day. There are five fundamental effects of laughter.

1. Bonding. The first fundamental effect is that laughter bonds teams. My definition of a team is two or more people with a common task.

If you have somebody, or a group of somebodies, that you can't get along with or who have problems getting along with each other, be it at home, or at work, or otherwise, there is a solution. Find something (not someone) that is just wrong, to laugh at. Make it an inside joke that you can get everyone to see the humor in. Now when you see each other, you smile and that overwhelming need to slap each other tends to subside.

I know most people would never actually choose to slap someone else. However, two people may snarl or have some other reaction instead. This will help to eliminate these reactions.

That smile, or that inside joke, now reminds you that you have something in common. It bonds the team and makes things run smoother.

2. Authority. The second fundamental effect of laughter is that it conveys authority. The first time I heard that, I said, "I don't think so." But the more I study it, the more I know it is true. Do you want to follow a person that has no sense of humor and is always grumbling? When somebody makes a mistake, they freak out, yell, and scream. Wouldn't you rather be around someone who has enough self-esteem that they can smile, and if they make a mistake quickly find a way to fix it? When you make a mistake, they say, "Okay let's fix it." You want to be around a person with enough self-esteem that they can roll with the punches and come back, smile and make it better next time.

3. Feels Good! The third fundamental to laughter is that it produces the endorphins in the brain that are similar to morphine. If you've ever had a day at work where you just needed some drugs, you can now get them fast, for free, and not go to jail for it.

Seriously, like a good round of exercise, laughter produces endorphins. Those same endorphins lower the heart rate, lower the blood pressure and improve the immune system. The third fundamental effect then, is that it helps to make you healthier.

4. Working, Working, Working... The fourth fundamental effect of laughter is that it improves productivity. There have been many studies that show this to be true. People who can have fun at work, can smile, who enjoy their jobs, and can generate a little happiness, are much more productive than the people who do not. In fact, companies that have fun, that encourage fun, that encourage smiling, encourage a warm welcoming environment where things are a lot happier, find that their productivity skyrockets: it goes through the roof.

A word of caution however, there is a distinction between fun and levity. Avoid levity. Levity conveys the perception that you don't take things seriously. Laughter and fun can be integrated into even the most serious conversation. Levity cannot.

Laugh often and encourage others to laugh as well.

5. The Long View. The fifth fundamental effect of laughter is that it helps to put things into perspective. It also helps to open your mind to other possibilities! Because, in most cases, laughter comes from looking at the same thing from a different view, it opens up your mind to other ways of seeing things and helps you view things with a clearer perspective.

This one really worried me years ago, because I was one of those people that didn't laugh. In fact, I was one of those people who had forgotten to tell their face they were having a good day. I had a friend who was a psychologist tell me, "You know, dear, it is okay if you don't laugh as long as you smile for 20 minutes a day. Because smiling for 20 minutes is the equivalent of laughing for five."

You know, it took a while, but I was able to make myself smile for 20 minutes. Now, I smile all the time. I don't even know I am smiling most of the time. Smiling now comes naturally for me. If you smile for 20 minutes or laugh for five in a row, it will eliminate stress faster than anything else that you can do.

Thirsty?

Here's another ICS: Drink water. Eight ounces of water in five minutes produces two endorphins that lower your stress levels. Pretty good right? Yes, eight ounces of water—in five minutes—two endorphins will lower your stress levels.

Any Thoughts?

The last one I'll tell you about is meditation. We don't typically think of meditating as an instant calming sequence but it is. I am not telling you to start sitting in the corner with your legs crossed and your arms in a lotus going "OMMMM" for two or three hours.

That may be a perception of how meditation works. If you truly understand meditation, you know this is not how it goes. AND if you do have the discipline and the time for a two hour session, that's great! If you do, you most likely won't need to worry about taking any stress management classes. Most of us don't have that kind of discipline and don't see the need to take the time.

However, meditation is invaluable. I suggest you plan for an instant calming sequence of meditation for 30 seconds to a minute and a half a day. The secret is in knowing what to do.

Meditation is not a blank mind, so I am not going to tell you to let your mind go blank. That's actually not very likely, and little value comes from it. We simply can't let our mind go 100% blank as we normally think of it. So, instead, spend 30 seconds refocused on something that makes you smile. Focus to the point that nothing else intrudes for that entire time. When your mind wanders, you channel it in the direction of your focus. So, here's your first mediation assignment: Ponder and answer this, "What makes me smile? What makes me laugh?"

I like to go to YouTube and watch children laughing. You can easily search "laughing" and get thousands of videos to choose from. The videos range from infants to 95 year-olds. There are countless videos of individuals and groups laughing. I'll watch them just laugh and laugh, until I have tears running down my face. Some people like the cats that are trapped in paper bags and can't get out. Some people think that is just mean. My kids liked Llamas in Hats or Charlie the Unicorn. "Charlie!" That one is just freaky to me.

Regardless, find what makes you smile and what makes you laugh. I like children, so I will pick clips or thoughts of children laughing. Once you have several examples, find a time and place where you can let your mind focus on the laughter.

Let's practice now. Set your timer for 30 seconds. If you don't know what makes you smile, you can borrow mine this time. For 30 seconds imagine a small child laughing. Not ready for 30 whole seconds?

Okay, try it first for just ten seconds. Set the timer. Ready? Go!

Okay, that was only ten seconds. When I do this with a group of people, I always see shoulders begin to relax and smiles start to spread across faces. Some people will start to laugh in ten seconds or less–in ten seconds!

So, for real, do it for 30 seconds. If, in ten seconds you already begin to relax and eliminate some of your stress, imagine what you can do in 30 seconds.

My suggestion is that from now on, every day, when you pull into the parking lot at work, close your eyes and imagine something that makes you laugh or smile. Then, every day when you get into your car in the parking lot after work, before you put your car into gear, pause, close your eyes and imagine something that makes you laugh or smile. Even better still, once you get home and are in your driveway, close your eyes and imagine something that makes you laugh or smile.

Remember to set your timer. Just because you can fall asleep in 30 seconds or less doesn't mean you have to prove it!

If you choose to do this, and all life is a result of choices you make, you will start having much more productive days at work and more enjoyable evenings at home.

Remember the Gratitudes? Laughing reminds you to be grateful. You see humor in most events. That is what allows you to develop that positive attitude.

For now, 30 seconds at a time is all I am asking. Do this for 30 seconds, two times a day, and you will have taken an entire minute, one 86,400th (1/86,400) of your time today to make your entire world a better place! That is what I call a great return on an investment!

Now, here's one that may sound strange. I am also going to tell you to stop listening to the news. This is especially important on the way to work or on your way home from work. That just puts you in a negative mood. Everything is sensationalized and there is rarely anything you can do about it. Talk radio is just as bad. Have you felt the "spin up" you get listening to talk radio? Doom, Gloom, Desperation, and Desolation.

Simply put, they cause you additional stress that is not needed, wanted, or useful in your life. Unless your job revolves around knowing the media's spin on current events, you simply don't need the stress.

And where do you get the good stuff? You create good stuff. Your life, your family, your friends are the good stuff. The good stuff never came from the TV news, newspapers, negative radio, or most internet sites. You don't really need them.

Take a break from doom and gloom.

Find the positive programs on TV, the radio, and the Internet. They will lift you, inspire productivity, and move you toward positive change. Spend a small portion of your day with them.

Trust me, somebody will tell you when the world is ending. Odds are the news won't carry it until it's over. So, instead of listening to the news, listen to a comedian, listen to a good positive book on tape, and listen to uplifting music (yes, it exists). Listen to something that will make you smile. This will help you with your meditation as well.

Simple

Instant calming sequences can be done very quickly and they will eliminate stress temporarily. The longer you continue, the more you learn to ignore and acclimate. If you do them long enough, you can eliminate the stress entirely.

CHAPTER 17

Long Term Fixes

L ET'S TALK ABOUT SOME OF THE LONG-TERM FIXES AND SOME OF the preventive measures for stress.

The Big Picture

Here's your first long term-fix: remember the big picture. The big picture is not the flat tire. The flat tire is simply a momentary thing. You know how to determine the big picture. You've heard it over and over. The question to ask at that point is, "Is it going to matter ten years from now?" Or, "Twenty years from now is it going to make the world a different place?"

You and I hear these things quite often. We have a tendency to blow right past that annoying question. But it's still a great and valid question! Will it really matter? Will it?

We often lose sight of the real root level follow-up question, "If it will matter in 20 years, is there anything that I should be doing to change or solidify that future outcome?" If this is something for which you have absolutely no control, and which you cannot plan for in any fashion, quit worrying about it. Don't let it upset you (as if any thought had that ability now), and put it out of your mind.

When I was first married, many, many years ago, we were both in school. My ex didn't have a job and we didn't have enough money to buy milk, let alone eggs. We went hungry a good portion of the time.

I had been able to take on an extra side job to bring in some grocery money. I remember my first payday. I had earned fifty bucks in cash. I was so excited because I was going to go to the grocery store as soon as I got home. I put the $50 bill in my front coat pocket and zipped the pocket shut. When I got home, the money was gone and I was devastated. I felt like the world was going to come to an end. I was sick about losing it. I was distraught at the thought of another month without real grocery shopping. To this day, I don't know if I lost the money or if someone stole it.

But that wasn't the big picture. At the time, the big picture for me, was that I actually thought we were going to starve to death. We didn't eat a lot. Our stomachs growled quite a bit, but, truthfully, we were okay.

Here it is 30 some odd years later and I must admit I am so glad I am not going through that now. However, in the big picture that $50 does not now, and truly did not then, really matter. It was very uncomfortable at the time, but IN THE LONG TERM, it really didn't matter. Money is just money. It is a means to an end. It comes and it goes. Ten years from now you won't miss what you don't have now. Twenty years from now, you will say, hmmm, it might have been nice to have that boat, or that car, but you know what, it's okay because my choice was to have other things.

So keep the big picture in mind. If what's happening doesn't change that picture, don't sweat it.

Here's the universal mantra, "This too, shall pass." And the reason it will pass is because you will take control of your life, accept the changes, create your opportunities, and make the best of your challenges.

Don't Take on the World's Problems

Here's another long-term fix: Don't take on too much.

Here's another one that seems counter-intuitive, "Stop being so selfish." How can you be selfish by trying to do too much?

When we take on too much, what we are saying, essentially to the world is, "I don't trust you and you can't do it as well as I can," or, "I am not going to give you the opportunity to grow, prosper and/or shine in your strengths." It sounds really selfish when you hear it that way doesn't it? Well, it is.

I mentioned earlier that we were dorm parents. We had the dormitory where the girls ate in the cafeteria because most of their parents knew their child could not take care of themselves or survive on their own. Sadly, most were right.

We had 210 girls in our dorm at any given time and approximately 190 of them truly were not capable of taking care of themselves. Why? They had never been given the opportunity to do it. Somebody, every time, had always done it for them. It was easier, it was faster, it was quicker, and it was better (for everyone else).

These poor young ladies did not know what that large piece of cloth was that had elastic around the corners. When you explained it was a fitted sheet they were confused, "What's that?"

I'd tell them, "It goes on the bed, it is the one that you sleep on top of."

Then they would say, "Oh! You have to put those on the bed?"

How about this? "What does it mean when it says don't wash colors and the whites together?" Well, it means if you wash your red shirt with your white socks you are going to have pink socks. They simply did not understand these things.

We had girls who did not know how to make ice cubes because they had never been given the opportunity to grow, progress, and to shine in their strengths or to even attempt to find some strengths. Moral of the story: Stop taking on so much, and start allowing other people to do things.

We have all heard it is better to give than to receive. But if from time to time you are not receiving, you are being selfish because you are not allowing others the opportunity to give. While, to balance the universe, you must give, give a lot, and give often, also be sure to allow others the opportunity to give and receive the blessings from that effort.

Every sage through the recorded history of humankind, every individual growth mentor, every motivational speaker, and yes, most authors like me, will tell you that the first order of humankind is to be of service, to love people, and to be genuinely involved in good works. That is the basis of most religions and almost all new age thinking. The closer you come to this element of perfection, both giving and receiving, the more valuable you become as an individual and the less stress you incur.

Remember, stress is generated when your choices are at odds with your core values. You know your core values. Stay in line and Karma will take care of the rest.

PARTY!

Here's another long-term fix. If work stresses you out, then spend time away from work. Spend time with your friends, with your family, with total strangers or even completely alone. If your friends and family stress you out, find new friends and avoid your family. Okay, maybe you can't avoid your family, but do find new friends and find a way to bridge the gap with your family. There truly is no reason in the long run to have ill feelings with family. Forgive and forget, fully and honestly.

Find people that are positive and pleasant to be around. Find people that actually lift your spirits and make you feel better. Ones that actually like some of the same things you do. For you non-joiners, stretch your social skills and talk to strangers. Everyone has a story. Everyone is a potential friend. Find someone sitting alone in a restaurant or bar or on a park bench and say, "Hi." If they bite, you can decide if that's okay.

The old adage goes, "You are the average of your best three friends." Choose them wisely.

Take Care

Another long-term fix is to take care of yourself physically as well as spiritually.

We all know to exercise, eat right, and drink lots of water. Your life will be much better on a daily basis if you follow these basic rules. Exercise generates endorphins. You literally get a physical high when you exercise. Your outlook changes, your spirits raise, and you just simply feel better.

This is also a major component of your spiritual well-being. It sets you on the path to be able to take care of yourself spiritually. I am not saying that you must believe in a particular religion or God. That is up to you and your belief system.

What I am saying is that in order for you to believe that things can be okay you must exercise a hope and a faith that things will eventually turn out right. This is where you can believe in religion that teaches a reward for good deeds, the laws of the universe, the laws of attraction, in Karma, in fate. The requirement here is that you remove the self-centered, selfish notion that you are somehow the center of the universe. You are not and never will be. Do you want your contribution to be to build and bless humanity, or do you want to leave a legacy of moral poverty? It is your choice.

Having said that, you must always allow yourself to have just a little hope and faith that things will be okay. Here, you hold to that hope and faith that you will find the end of the tunnel and then look for the light to see you through. So, take care of yourself both physically and spiritually.

CHAPTER 18

Prevention Is Better Than Treatment

OKAY, HOW ABOUT SOME PREVENTATIVE MEASURES FOR STRESS?

There's a Reason We Have Borders

Here's a great one. Set boundaries for yourself, for your 2%ers, and sometimes for the 8%ers. To set boundaries that remove the 8%ers that are having a bad day, tell them something like this, "You are entitled to a bad day but you are not entitled to treat me this way when you have one."

With the 2%ers remember, it is your reaction that they get their jollies from. Don't play their game. Set boundaries with consequences you are willing to follow up on.

My dad, may he rest in peace, was a true 2%er. I truly loved the man. He had great traits and qualities. People loved and adored him. But boy, if he could upset you, and get your goat (a euphemism for annoy to a point of tears), he was in seventh heaven. My mom used to say, "He can't get your goat if you hide your goat."

She was right, of course, but I had a hard time hiding my goat because he knew all the trigger points and buttons to push. When he would push them, I would react. Okay, usually I would overreact!

While my dad did delight in upsetting people, I wouldn't go as far as to say he was sadistic, perhaps misguided and following parental guidelines he had learned in his own youth.

Regardless, I seemed to be one of his favorite sparring partners. One day my oldest brother said, "He only does it because he knows it upsets you."

What he did to upset me the most, I believe probably would have upset you too:

In his latter years, my Dad had very poor health and had become legally blind. He had only his peripheral vision. He could see, but it was like he had two hands right in front of his face at all times. His real vision was exclusively a small circle around the sides. He really should not have been driving.

At that time, I was married with small children. A couple times a month, I'd take my family and would drive the four and a half hours to visit Mom and Dad because they both needed help. Mom worked full-time and also took care of Dad full-time. My siblings and I would take turns going down and helping them out. When I would go down to their home, my dad loved to sneak my kids to his car and drive to the grocery store to get ice cream cones.

That simply was not EVER okay, period, end of story. Having begun my journey into emotional power, I thought I would set some boundaries. At least, I had that intention.

I screamed. I cussed. I begged. I pleaded. I bargained. I negotiated. But I didn't actually set a boundary. Real boundaries come with consequences I was willing to follow through with. What I really ended up with were shallow and hollow threats. All I did was vent without resolution.

My brother again, would say, "You know he only does this because it upsets you so much."

I would say "Well, it would upset you too if he took your children."

He said, "You're right! Have you noticed he doesn't? He doesn't because he knows when I say no, I mean no." He continued, "You have tried to set boundaries, but you are not willing to follow through on the consequences; therefore, there is no real boundary. You draw lines in the sand and then hand Dad a fan so he can blow the line away. You have to figure out what you really want, what you are willing to do to get it and then draw the line in quick drying cement. Then, if you must, you may hand him the fan! He can help you dry it. If you later find it's not the line you want, fill it in and drill or chisel out a better line. Sand isn't for real; cement is."

I thought long and hard about the lines I had drawn. I asked myself what consequences was I willing to set that would be strong enough that he would take seriously but that I would still have the strength myself to follow through with. The real issue was, and always has been, regardless of his faults, he was my dad, and I loved him. He was the one that set boundaries for me my entire life. That made it all the more difficult to set boundaries for him.

It took time, but I came up with one. I went to their home and said, "Dad I love you and I respect you. I know you love me. I need you to respect my wishes. We've talked at great length about how inappropriate it is to take the children in the car. I am no longer willing to play games about this. My children's lives may hang in the balance. So from this moment forward, if you as much as go up and down the driveway with them in the car, we will leave for six months, and not return during that time. With your health, that period of time could be the rest of your lifetime. Please, do not take my kids in the car ever again."

Do you know what that man did? Yep! He took my kids out to the car, and he drove up and down the driveway. He did not even leave the property. He just went up and down that driveway.

Now what do you think my gut instinct as his child was? Obviously, it was to give him another chance. He was after all only pushing a little, and my kids were not really in any danger with that antic.

I really thought about going out and saying, "Dad, I am serious. If you do it again…" But I had set a consequence. I had finally drawn the line in cement. And, even though he didn't fully appreciate or understand that it was cement this time, my choices were to allow him to completely ignore my wishes for the rest of his life, or to stand firm in my decision. This was exactly the scenario I had warned against. Now, I had to follow up on the consequences so he understood the seriousness of my request.

I took a deep breath, went out and said with my "Please pass the butter" voice, "Dad, I love you and I respect you. I know you love me. I am sorry to see you don't respect me. Come on kids we are going home. Dad, stay healthy because I do want to see you again."

Those were the longest six months of my life. Now, he did live for an additional ten years, thank goodness, but in those six months, I got calls from my mom that started with, "You are killing your father." I also got calls from my dad starting with, "You are killing your mother." I got calls from my siblings, "We need your help. Get down there and help out."

But, I had set a boundary with a consequence. I had to follow up on it. As tough as it was, I followed through with it.

Six months later, we went back, and I sat down with my dad and said, "Dad, I love you and I respect you. I know you love me. I need you to respect my wishes. From now on, when I say no, I mean no."

And he said, "Okay." And he never took my children again. Of course, he started taking my sister's kids, but that is another story.

Let me make this clear to you, you want to avoid behaviors, not people. Sometimes you may end up avoiding people to avoid the behavior. I understand that. But over the long run, that is not best for you or the one with the behavior.

You must keep in mind that it is not the person who drives you crazy; it is always their behavior that drives you crazy. Let me tell you a secret, most people that drive you crazy are mirroring some behavior of your own. You find it annoying in yourself and react poorly to anyone else who displays it.

Are They Doing This on Purpose?

If Ted is clicking his pen on and off, on and off, on and off, and it drives you insane, then if Ted quits the job and they hire Suzy, and Suzy clicks her pen on and off, on and off, on and off, she is going to drive you insane too.

It is not Ted or Suzy that drives you insane, it is their behavior. The only way to work with the behavior is to point out that it is bothersome, inappropriate, or irksome and ask them to stop doing it. Then if they don't, you have to ask yourself if you are willing to let it go or if you are willing to remove yourself from the situation.

Avoid behaviors not people. And keep this in mind, if it's not illegal, immoral, or life threatening, it's probably an acceptable behavior for some people. Often what upsets one person another one finds comforting. This circles back to the 98%ers who are not intentionally trying to annoy you.

Condition yourself to think, "I wonder if that gives him comfort or makes her happy" instead of "I hate that sound." Just remember the key is not always for someone else to change, though sometimes that may be the right answer. The key just might be for you to change your perception of the behavior and your perception of the person.

Focus on the Positive

Our final long-term fix for stress is to focus more on what is going right than on what is going wrong.

Have the gratitude journal, meditate, laugh, laugh, laugh, laugh. These are some great long-term fixes and preventive measures. When you follow these, you will find your stress levels go down immensely and stay down more often than not.

Remember, with every situation, there is a positive side. Even when things are bleak and desperate, this too shall pass. Always remember that. The only thing in this world that is permanent is death. In many cultures, even this is viewed as a transition to a new beginning. In all situations you will come through the dark tunnel stronger and wiser as you focus on gratitude.

So, optimist or pessimist: Which is better? Frankly, optimist is the correct answer. If you aren't one, start practicing. You don't have to be a Suzie Sweetheart, but smiling, being kind to small children and animals, and caring and helping even when no one is looking will completely change your life for the better. Be an optimist. It's the same effort with much larger benefits.

CHAPTER 19

Plan Your Life

I N THIS CHAPTER WE ARE GOING TO WRAP EVERYTHING TOGETHER and talk about the principle of "Plan your life, don't let life plan you."

This single concept will help you with all aspects of emotional power. It will help you with your emotion management. It will help you with your awareness. It will help you with your attitude and your empathy. It will help you be more socially skilled.

Where Are You Headed?

There are steps. Everything has steps. The old joke is very true:

Question: How do you eat an elephant?

Answer: One bite at a time.

The first thing to understand is that the only way you can truly plan your life is to actually have some type of personal/family mission, vision, values and goal statements and a motto to live by. Once you know what is important and where you want to end up, you can then plan your life to fulfill them.

At work, many of us have mission statements. That is how the company sees getting from where it is now to where it is going. It is how it knows when it arrives. The bosses have mapped out both the end result (the goal) and the way to get there, hopefully with your input.

But, how many of you have done the same thing for yourself or with your families? If a business, to which you are really not related, feels the need for a mission statement and wants you to understand and promote it, don't the people who mean the most to you in the world deserve the same thing?

Do you have family mission statements or personal mission statements? I have talked to literally tens of thousands of people about this and only a handful of them have a family and/or a personal mission statement. For the rest, I must ask, "How are you going to get where you want to go if you don't know where it is you want to go and how you are going to get there?"

Motto Lotto

I will be honest with you; I am not great at personal mission statements myself. I am much better with a motto.

Here are a couple examples:

- Simple: "Provide an environment of warmth and comfort to all who enter my home or office."
- Or one that makes you think, like my husband's: "All things in moderation, especially moderation."
- Perhaps one that serves as both a motto and a goal, like my sister Heather's: "Leave a legacy of love, learning and family values."

Inheritance or Legacy?

So, should you leave an inheritance? I don't know. But I do know that you should definitely plan to leave a legacy. An inheritance is what you leave FOR other people. A legacy is what you leave IN other people

An inheritance is just stuff. A legacy is something you can build upon. It is a way of life, a point of view, an understanding. It is a very strong and lifelong commitment.

For my sister Heather to live her motto, she constantly weighed her choices and actions against that simple, yet profound motto. If it was consistent with love, learning and family values, Heather was all over it. If it were contrary to it, she would avoid it like the plague. If it had nothing to do with her motto, she might get to it she might not. That is how she chose to live. She took her four core values and made them the focus of her life.

What were her core values? Love, learning, family values, and leaving a legacy. If she were to write on the paper with the four sections, I know this is what she would write down.

Meet Heather

You should know Heather. All Heather wanted to do was to grow up, get married, and have lots of babies. She grew up, got out of high school, and immediately got married, but she didn't have lots of babies. In fact, for five years, she didn't have any. She had no problem getting pregnant, but it was the carrying to term that simply didn't work and gave her heartache.

I'll be honest here. I'm pretty sure that I would have been angry at God, the universe and whomever else I thought had a part in this. But she would say, "Karen, Karen, Karen… being upset about this is not going to help me carry a child to term. Being resentful is like taking poison and waiting for the other person to die. Nothing is going to change there. I choose to be happy. I may have a heavy heart, sure, but that doesn't mean I can't have a happy life. I–choose–to–be–happy!"

11 Times

She had 11 miscarriages the first five years of her marriage. Eleven. Like I said, she had no problem getting pregnant. She did have a real hard time keeping the child. Now, that would really have stressed me out. It would have made me, well, far more than emotional. I don't know that I would have chosen well if I had to handle all that she went through. She, on the other hand, chose to be happy and truly was happy.

You know what she did in those five years? She wrote children songs, poems, and books. She played with everybody else's kids. She found out more about her situation and medical condition so that she could help other people who might have to go through similar situations. She solidified what family values meant to her. She had a heavy heart, she wanted a baby more than anything else but she was happy because she chose to be happy.

Where Are You Going?

You choose your path in life. You choose what you are going to do every moment of the day, from this moment forward. You always have. You see, the only difference is that Heather planned life instead of letting her life plan her. She had road-blocks, bumps and a few potholes, but she knew the path she chose to walk. She saw the long view and didn't let those minor details get in her way.

Happily, she did finally get pregnant with little Michael Ryan. He was the cutest baby you could ever hope to see. Well, because of complications with the pregnancy she ended up in bed. I know this can stress you out and make you highly emotional. With my last pregnancy I, too, ended up in bed. When you are stuck in bed, you are bored, you are lonely, you are tired, you are uncomfortable. Besides, those floors needed to be vacuumed and nobody could vacuum them as good as I could. I wonder why nobody wanted to come visit me when I was in bed. But everybody wanted to go see Heather.

I remember that first day I went over there, and I started with the, "Oh, you poor thing. This bed is going to kill you."

She went, "Whoa, whoa, Karen, complaining about the bed being uncomfortable is not going to make the bed any more comfortable. All it is going to do is solidify in my mind that I am uncomfortable. I either buy a new bed, or I get pillows and fluff them up, or I focus on something to let the time go by quickly."

Right! SHE chose to be happy. You know what she did while she was sick in bed with that pregnancy? She wrote children songs, poems and books, she listened to everything she could get her hands on, books on tape, positive motivational things, she read books, she read parenting magazines. She called other people she said, "Hey, I am in bed anyway, is there anything I can look up for you on the Internet?" She was a complete and total delight to be around and everybody went to visit her so she wasn't bored and lonely like I was. Go figure! She chose to be happy. She chose to live her life according to love, learning and family values.

The Family Began

Little Michael Ryan was finally born. But unfortunately he was one month early, exactly to the due date. Because he was a month early, and because of complications with the pregnancy, he ended up in the hospital the first three weeks of his life. Now, I am pretty sure that I would have lost it at this point. I would have said, "I stayed in bed, I did what you ask me to do. I was happy, I helped others, and I, I, I...."

"I" would have really lost it. But as we have said over and over, and as Heather said, "Karen, Karen, Karen, I choose to be happy, I choose to love my son starting now, not later. I choose to enjoy every moment

I have with him and not to waste these precious moments. I choose not to stress out about him being in the hospital because that is not going to change him being here. In fact, it will most likely make his stay longer. He will feel my stress and it will prevent him from healing as quickly."

During those first three weeks she spent in the hospital, she gave her time, her energy and her positive thoughts to her son. She spent her time singing and playing with Michael in his little incubator. When he was sleeping, she would go to the children's ward and read to them. She would go to the geriatric ward, and talk to them about how their day was going. She wrote love letters to her friends and family. Oh, and scrap booking! No kidding. She had Michael's first scrapbook done the day before he turned one month old. And she had completed not just one, but three, one for herself, one for her mother-in-law and one for my mother. Now, seriously, his first scrapbook finished the day before he turned one month old! My youngest child is a grown, married man, and I have not yet started his. Something is seriously wrong with this picture.

The Trip

Because of Dad's health, Mom and Dad didn't travel much, and they had scheduled all of Dad's appointments at the VA hospital close to where we lived for January 11th, Michael's due date because they wanted to be there when he was born.

And so on January 11th, his one month birthday, and his actual due date, Mom and Dad drove the four-and-a-half hours, and set up for the week at my brother's home. Heather gathered up Michael, the scrapbooks and a few other items because she and Michael were going to go back home with our parents and spend a couple of weeks. Excited to see them and introduce Michael to our parents, her little family headed to my brother's home. As Heather and her husband drove up through the canyon, a young woman decided to pass on a blind curve while speeding.

Bam!

Heather and Michael were killed instantly.

I don't tell you this to shock you or to upset you. I tell you this because Heather chose to be happy no matter what she had going on in her life.

Did she have a heavy heart? Oh, quite a bit of the time, but she lived her life according to her plan to leave a legacy of love, learning, and family values.

The Legacy

And, she left that legacy of love, learning, and family values. When we think of her, we don't think of her dishes being dirty, because who cares? Or that she rarely kept a job for more than six months, sometimes by choice, sometimes not. I mean, really, is it important? Nor do we think about, as she lovingly and jokingly would say, "My body by McDonalds."

Those things don't matter. What we do think about is love. Her love, her example, and her obvious love and care for everyone she met.

The day after she died, I got my last love letter from her in the mail. True story!

When I think of learning from Heather, here are a few things she taught:

- **Values**: She helped me solidify the value and importance of learning something new every single day.
- **Legacy**: She solidified learning as a lifestyle in my children.
- **Love**: She taught my children the love of knowledge. She shared her love with them, and taught them how to share with others.
- Family Values: She helped me solidify what family values meant to me.

Her funeral was one of the largest ones ever in our metropolitan area that didn't involve a dignitary. It was amazing how many people she had touched in her short life. The number of people she had lifted, just a little, and loved a lot. Over 2,000 people came to say good bye to her and little Michael. Every story was the same, "I met your sister because I needed to. She had more love for everyone in the world than I thought was possible. She was my angel, my guide, and my mentor. She was genuinely loving, caring, and wanted nothing but the best for me. I loved her for that."

What a Legacy! We may never measure up to hers. However, we can measure up to our own if we have a plan. You need a plan.

The Plan

Please learn to plan your life! Choose a path. Walk the path. Robert Frost wrote, "The Road Not Taken." In it, he describes the benefit and joy of following your own path. You don't have to take the deserted path. However you do it, make it your path, regardless of the number of others taking it. When you plan your life, there is no one else to blame. You become responsible.

Heather was a woman of true emotional power. She knew, without a doubt, she was responsible for herself first and primarily. She harnessed that Emotional Power and used it to build a better life for herself by building it for those in the world around her.

She lived, truly lived, the five components of emotional power.

Five Components of Emotional Power

Let's recap the five components through the story of Heather.

ONE: Awareness — She was aware of her emotions. She felt them fully she knew what emotions she was having and why she was having them. She purposefully chose the thoughts to have and had the thoughts that would take her where she wanted to go.

TWO: Attitude — She kept a good attitude even through heavy-hearted times. She didn't just believe; she knew things would always turn out alright.

THREE: Empathy — She had empathy for herself and for others. She allowed herself to feel sorrow and pain. And positively, she looked at it as a temporary state that would end as she shaped her own future. To her, sorrow and/or pain was simply another emotion she knew she was entitled to have. Like Victor Frankl in the prison camp, realizing that your reaction to the emotion is the key to your happiness, was a lesson she learned early. She did not need sorrow to be a defining mark to make her way in life. She allowed others this same opportunity.

FOUR: Social Skills — She was socially skilled. She knew how to get along with others and how to put them in the midst of happiness with her. She was aware of their needs and met them without denying her own. She was positive, assertive, and firm in her convictions. She didn't allow anyone, including her family, to rain on her parade. She eloquently communicated her convictions.

She took time to understand the other person and put them at ease, without personal judgment.

FIVE: Management — She managed the way she dealt with things because she planned her life instead of letting life plan her. She knew her core values, put them first, and let everything else fall into the proper place.

Plan Your Life Worksheet

Mission:

Vision:

Core Values statement:

Goals:

Motto to live by:

Plan your life! Don't let life plan you!

Epilogue

I'VE FINALLY PASSED THE HALF-WAY POINT IN MY LIFE. I PLAN TO LIVE to 100. Now, with my husband, that may be what we really want to do. There are so many great adventures, so many ways to be of service, and so many things yet to learn that it will take another 50 years to get a good start on them.

During my life to this point, I've been amazed at how smart older people have become (smile and nod here please). When I was 20, anyone over 30 just didn't understand. When I was 30, 40 was over the hill and "those people" simply couldn't relate to my life, or so I thought. I've just passed 50, and I'm amazed at the knowledge, wisdom, and true love that we possess. We've made the mistakes. Many of us have learned from them. Some of us make them over and over as a reminder of just how bad that choice is.

I also now realize how much young people can learn from the older ones. Every one of them has had to make decisions the young are just facing. Each of them came up with a solution that worked. And now, I'm in awe of the long-term vision older people have. Most of them can tell you, without a shadow of a doubt, what lies on a path you may choose.

I think, should I live to be 100 years old, I would want to spend my time helping others to learn to choose wisely and enjoy a life of mostly correct choices. Correct for them, in their lives, at that point for them. The older people in your life (regardless how old you are now) truly want the best for you. Some of them, when urged to share, may actually be valuable to you. Give it a try.

Remember, service and love are truly the most important, and only Legacies of value you can leave for those you love.

A Challenge

My hope and challenge for you is that you will find the emotional power within you and that you will plan your life around that power and not let life plan you and/or have it just happen to you.

You know the skills now. All that remains is to exercise. Exercise faith and hope that what you have learned actually works. Exercise yourself in the activities you've been taught. Exercise your relationships. Exercise your emotions. Bring calm, quiet, and peace to your mind and soul.

And as you do this, share your new, better, happier life with anyone who will listen.

Now, turn to page one, start reading again and implement your plan!

Bibliography

1. K. Luan Phan, MD, Tor D. Wager, PhD, Stephan F. Taylor, MD, and Israel Liberzon, MD. Functional Neuroimaging Studies of Human Emotions. CNS Spectrums – April 2004:
   http://www.columbia.edu/cu/psychology/tor/Papers/Phan_Wager_2004_CNS_Emotion_review.pdf

2. Hubert H. Humphrey. (n.d.). BrainyQuote.com. Retrieved June 25, 2014, from BrainyQuote.com Web site: http://www.brainyquote.com/quotes/quotes/h/huberthhu103505.html

3. Frankl, Victor E., Man's Search for Meaning. Retrieved June 25, 2014, from GoodReads.com Web Site: https://www.goodreads.com/work/quotes/3389674

4. Victor Frankl, quoted from Wikipedia. http://en.wikipedia.org/wiki/Viktor_Frankl

5. Frankl, Victor E., Man's Search for Meaning. Retrieved June 25, 2014, from GoodReads.com Web Site: https://www.goodreads.com/work/quotes/3389674

6. Stress: A Cause of Cancer? By LISA HURT KOZAROVICH, http://psychcentral.com/lib/stress-a-cause-of-cancer/000754

7. Heart disease in women: Understand symptoms and risk factors, The Mayo Clinic Staff. http://www.mayoclinic.org/diseases-conditions/heart-disease/in-depth/heart-disease/art-20046167

8. Frost, Robert (1874-1963). Mountain Interval, 1920. "The Road Not Taken." http://www.bartleby.com/119/1.html

Sociable Peacock

Core Motivation: Fun

Fear: Not Being Recognized

Motto: Get Noticed

Natural Talents: Enthusiasm and Optimism

Communication Preference:
Let them know it's making them look good
Appreciate and Validate them

Likes: Popularity, Attention, Constant Validation, Challenges, Adventure, Spontaneity, and Excitement

Dislikes: Waiting, Slow-to-Get-Things-Done People, Convention, Indecision, and Lack of Enthusiasm

Strengths: Socially Skilled, Outgoing, Persuasive, Risk Taker, Competitive, Confident, Pursues Change, Inspiring, Open, and Direct

Limitations: Risk Taker, Reactive, Dominating, Abrasive, Impatient, Restless, Overbearing, Pushy, Intimidating

Dark Lord Peacocks: Politically Incorrect, Lazy, Irresponsible, Inept, Aimless

A saying they would agree with:
All Work and No Play is Missing the Point!

Director Lion

Core Motivation: Power

Fear: Being taken advantage of

Motto: Get it done (NOW!)

Natural Talents:
Leadership
Vision

Communication Preference:
Facts only
Get to the point – get out

Likes: Control, Responsibility, Loyalty, Quick Decisions, and Mastery

Dislikes: Irreverence, Laziness, Slow-acting People, and Indecision

Strengths: Ambitious, Assertive, Confident, Decisive, Dependable, Goal oriented, Practical, Proactive, Responsible, Self-determined, Self-motivated, Very direct

Limitations: Always Right, Argumentative, Critical, Distant, Dogmatic, Impatient, Insensitive, Overly economical, Selfish, Stubborn, Unapproachable

Dark Side: Delegate, Demand, Cause stress in others, Task Dominant, More productive and successful, Overly aggressive

A saying they would agree with:
I'll try being nicer.... If you try being smarter!

Loyal Lamb

Core Motivation: Intimacy

Fear: Conflict

Motto: Get Along

Natural Talents: Quality and Service

Communication Preference:
Let them know how it affects others
Appreciation for their concern
Appreciation for all they do

Likes: Closeness, Affirmation, Kindness, Caring, Friends, and Family, Ethical behavior, Being understood, Being appreciated, Being accepted, Quality, Being secure

Dislikes: Egotism, Contention, Insensitivity, Insincerity

Strengths: Caring, Extremely helpful, Fabulous team players, Giving, Good friends, Good listeners, Intuitive, Kind, Loyal, Sincere, Thoughtful, Very Devoted

Limitations: Overly sensitive, Too hesitant, Passive, Too "other" oriented, Indecisive, Vulnerable, Self-righteous, Perfectionist, Worry prone, Unrealistic expectations

Dark Side: Can be the stalkers, Won't Trust, Excessive Worry, Depression, and Self-loathing

A saying they would agree with:
If you love someone, set them free. If they come back, they're yours. If not, hunt them down and kill them!

Analyst Owl

Core Motivation: Peace

Fear: Getting Reprimanded (negative feedback)

Motto: Get It Right!

Natural Talents: Clarity and Tolerance

Communication Preference:
All the facts
Details to support analysis
Validated research

Likes: Research, Information, Consistency, and Perfection

Dislikes: Arrogance, Unnecessary Risks, Carelessness, and Overly Assertive People

Strengths: Meticulous, Practical, Avoid Unnecessary Risks, Exacting, Factual, Reserved, and Have High Standards

Limitations: Perfectionists, Slow to Get Things Done, Loners, Passive/Aggressive, Withdrawn, Dull, and Know-it-All

Dark Side: Blow up from pent up emotions, Inappropriately Angry, Seemingly Strange

A saying they would agree with:
If I pretend to agree with you, will you go away?